SPECTRUM

Test Prep

Grade 3

SPECTRUM

Columbus, Ohio

Credits:
School Specialty Publishing Editorial/Art & Design Team
Vincent F. Douglas, *President*
Tracey E. Dils, *Publisher*
Phyllis Sibbing, B.S. Ed., *Project Editor*
Rose Audette, *Art Director*

Also Thanks to:
MaryAnne Nestor, Layout and Production
Jenny Campbell, Interior Illustration

Send all inquiries to:
School Specialty Publishing
8720 Orion Place
Columbus, OH 43240-2111

ISBN 1-57768-663-2

11 12 13 14 15 POH 11 10 09 08 07 06

Table of Contents

Just for Parents

For All Students

Kinds of Questions

Subject Help

Practice Test and Final Test

About the Tests

What Are Standardized Achievement Tests?

Achievement tests measure what children know in particular subject areas such as reading, language arts, and mathematics. They do not measure your child's intelligence or ability to learn.

When tests are standardized, or *normed,* children's test results are compared with those of a specific group who have taken the test, usually at the same age or grade.

Standardized achievement tests measure what children around the country are learning. The test makers survey popular textbook series, as well as state curriculum frameworks and other professional sources, to determine what content is covered widely.

Because of variations in state frameworks and textbook series, as well as grade ranges on some test levels, the tests may cover some material that children have not yet learned. This is especially true if the test is offered early in the school year. However, test scores are compared to those of other children who take the test at the same time of year, so your child will not be at a disadvantage if his or her class has not covered specific material yet.

Different School Districts, Different Tests

There are many flexible options for districts when offering standardized tests. Many school districts choose not to give the full test battery, but select certain content and scoring options. For example, many schools may test only in the areas of reading and mathematics. Similarly, a state or district may use one test for certain grades and another test for other grades. These decisions are often based on

the amount of time and money a district wishes to spend on test administration. Some states choose to develop their own statewide assessment tests.

On pages 6 and 7 you will find information about these five widely used standardized achievement tests:

- California Achievement Tests (CAT)
- Terra Nova/CTBS
- Iowa Test of Basic Skills (ITBS)
- Stanford Achievement Test (SAT9)
- Metropolitan Achievement Test (MAT).

However, this book contains strategies and practice questions for use with a variety of tests. Even if your state does not give one of the five tests listed above, your child will benefit from doing the practice questions in this book. If you're unsure about which test your child takes, contact your local school district to find out which tests are given.

Types of Test Questions

Traditionally, standardized achievements tests have used only multiple choice questions. Today, many tests may include constructed response (short answer) and extended response (essay) questions as well.

In addition, many tests include questions that tap students' higher-order thinking skills. Instead of simple recall questions, such as identifying a date in history, questions may require students to make comparisons and contrasts or analyze results among other skills.

What the Tests Measure

These tests do not measure your child's level of intelligence, but they do show how well your child knows material that he or she has learned and that is also covered on the tests. It's important to remember that some tests cover content that is not taught in your child's school or grade. In other instances, depending on when in the year the test is given, your child may not yet have covered the material.

If the test reports you receive show that your child needs improvement in one or more skill areas, you may want to seek help from your child's teacher and find out how you can work with your child to improve his or her skills.

California Achievement Tests (CAT/5)

What Is the *California Achievement Test?*

The *California Achievement Test* is a standardized achievement test battery that is widely used with elementary through high school students.

Parts of the Test

The CAT includes tests in the following content areas:

Reading
- Word Analysis
- Vocabulary
- Comprehension

Spelling

Language Arts
- Language Mechanics
- Language Usage

Mathematics

Science

Social Studies

Your child may take some or all of these subtests if your district uses the *California Achievement Test.*

Terra Nova/CTBS (Comprehensive Tests of Basic Skills)

What Is the *Terra Nova/CTBS?*

The *Terra Nova/Comprehensive Tests of Basic Skills* is a standardized achievement test battery used in elementary through high school grades.

While many of the test questions on the *Terra Nova* are in the traditional multiple choice form, your child may take parts of the *Terra Nova* that include some open-ended questions (constructed-response items).

Parts of the Test

Your child may take some or all of the following subtests if your district uses the *Terra Nova/CTBS:*

Reading/Language Arts
Mathematics
Science
Social Studies

Supplementary tests include:
- Word Analysis
- Vocabulary
- Language Mechanics
- Spelling
- Mathematics Computation

Critical thinking skills may also be tested.

Iowa Tests of Basic Skills (ITBS)

What Is the *ITBS?*

The *Iowa Test of Basic Skills* is a standardized achievement test battery used in elementary through high school grades.

Parts of the Test

Your child may take some or all of these subtests if your district uses the *ITBS*, also known as the *Iowa:*

Reading
- Vocabulary
- Reading Comprehension

Language Arts
- Spelling
- Capitalization
- Punctuation
- Usage and Expression

Math
- Concepts/Estimate
- Problems/Data Interpretation

Social Studies

Science

Sources of Information

Stanford Achievement Test (SAT9)

What Is the *Stanford Achievement Test?*

The *Stanford Achievement Test, Ninth Edition (SAT9)* is a standardized achievement test battery used in elementary through high school grades.

Note that the *Stanford Achievement Test (SAT9)* is a different test from the *SAT* used by high school students for college admissions.

While many of the test questions on the *SAT9* are in traditional multiple choice form, your child may take parts of the *SAT9* that include some open-ended questions (constructed-response items).

Parts of the Test

Your child may take some or all of these subtests if your district uses the *Stanford Achievement Test.*

Reading
- Vocabulary
- Reading Comprehension

Mathematics
- Problem Solving
- Procedures

Language Arts

Spelling

Study Skills

Listening

Critical thinking skills may also be tested.

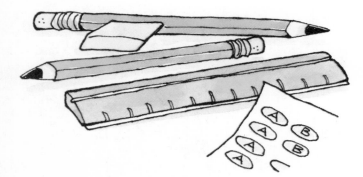

Metropolitan Achievement Test (MAT7 and MAT8)

What Is the *Metropolitan Achievement Test*?

The *Metropolitan Achievement Test* is a standardized achievement test battery used in elementary through high school grades.

Parts of the Test

Your child may take some or all of these subtests if your district uses the *Metropolitan Achievement Test*.

Reading
- Vocabulary
- Reading Comprehension

Math
- Concepts and Problem Solving
- Computation

Language Arts
- Pre-writing
- Composing
- Editing

Science
Social Studies
Research Skills
Thinking Skills
Spelling

Statewide Assessments

Today the majority of states give statewide assessments. In some cases these tests are known as *high-stakes assessments*. This means that students must score at a certain level in order to be promoted. Some states use minimum competency or proficiency tests. Often these tests measure more basic skills than other types of statewide assessments.

Statewide assessments are generally linked to state curriculum frameworks. Frameworks provide a blueprint, or outline, to ensure that teachers are covering the same curriculum topics as other teachers in the same grade level in the state. In some states, standardized achievement tests (such as the five described in this book) are used in connection with statewide assessments.

When Statewide Assessments Are Given

Statewide assessments may not be given at every grade level. Generally, they are offered at one or more grades in elementary school, middle school, and high school. Many states test at grades 4, 8, and 10.

State-by-State Information

You can find information about statewide assessments and curriculum frameworks at your state Department of Education Web site. To find the address for your individual state go to www.ed.gov, click on Topics A–Z, and then click on State Departments of Education. You will find a list of all the state departments of education, mailing addresses, and Web sites.

How to Help Your Child Prepare for Standardized Testing

Preparing All Year Round

Perhaps the most valuable way you can help your child prepare for standardized achievement tests is by providing enriching experiences. Keep in mind also, that test results for younger children are not as reliable as for older students. If a child is hungry, tired, or upset, this may result in a poor test score. Here are some tips on how you can help your child do his or her best on standardized tests.

Read aloud with your child. Reading aloud helps develop vocabulary and fosters a positive attitude toward reading. Reading together is one of the most effective ways you can help your child succeed in school.

Share experiences. Baking cookies together, planting a garden, or making a map of your neighborhood are examples of activities that help build skills that are measured on the tests such as sequencing and following directions.

Become informed about your state's testing procedures. Ask about or watch for announcements of meetings that explain about standardized tests and statewide assessments in your school district.

Talk to your child's teacher about your child's individual performance on these state tests during a parent-teacher conference.

Help your child know what to expect. Read and discuss with your child the test-taking tips in this book. Your child can prepare by working through a couple of strategies a day so that no practice session takes too long.

Help your child with his or her regular school assignments. Set up a quiet study area for homework. Supply this area with pencils, paper, markers, a calculator, a ruler, a dictionary, scissors, glue, and so on. Check your child's homework and offer to help if he or she gets stuck. But remember, it's your child's homework, not yours. If you help too much, your child will not benefit from the activity.

Keep in regular contact with your child's teacher. Attend parent-teacher conferences, school functions, PTA or PTO meetings, and school board meetings. This will help you get to know the educators in your district and the families of your child's classmates.

Learn to use computers as an educational resource. If you do not have a computer and Internet access at home, try your local library.

Remember—simply getting your child comfortable with testing procedures and helping him or her know what to expect can improve test scores!

Getting Ready for the Big Day

There are lots of things you can do on or immediately before test day to improve your child's chances of testing success. What's more, these strategies will help your child prepare him or herself for school tests, too, and promote general study skills that can last a lifetime.

Provide a good breakfast on test day.

Instead of sugar cereal, which provides immediate but not long-term energy, have your child eat a breakfast with protein or complex carbohydrates such as an egg, whole grain cereal or toast, or a banana-yogurt shake.

Promote a good night's sleep. A good night's sleep before the test is essential. Try not to overstress the importance of the test. This may cause your child to lose sleep because of anxiety. Doing some exercise after school and having a quiet evening routine will help your child sleep well the night before the test.

Assure your child that he or she is not expected to know all of the answers on the test. Explain that other children in higher grades may take the same test, and that the test may measure things your child has not yet learned in school. Help your child understand that you expect him or her to put forth a good effort—and that this is enough. Your child should not try to cram for these tests. Also avoid threats or bribes; these put undue pressure on children and may interfere with their best performance.

Keep the mood light and offer encouragement. To provide a break on test days, do something fun and special after school— take a walk around the neighborhood, play a game, read a favorite book, or prepare a special snack together. These activities keep your child's mood light—even if the testing sessions have been difficult—and show how much you appreciate your child's effort.

Taking Standardized Tests

No matter what grade you're in, this is information you can use to prepare for standardized tests. Here is what you'll find:

- Test-taking tips and strategies to use on test day and year-round.
- Important terms to know for Language Arts, Reading, Math, Science, and Social Studies.
- A checklist of skills to complete to help you understand what you need to know in Language Arts, Reading Comprehension, Writing, and Math.
- General study/homework tips.

By opening this book, you've already taken your first step towards test success. The rest is easy—all you have to do is get started!

What You Need to Know

There are many things you can do to increase your test success. Here's a list of tips to keep in mind when you take standardized tests—and when you study for them, too.

Keep up with your school work. One way you can succeed in school and on tests is by studying and doing your homework regularly. Studies show that you remember only about one-fifth of what you memorize the night before a test. That's one good reason not to try to learn it all at once! Keeping up with your work throughout the year will help you remember the material better. You also won't be as tired or nervous as if you try to learn everything at once.

Feel your best. One of the ways you can do your best on tests and in school is to make sure your body is ready. To do this, get a good night's sleep each night and eat a healthy breakfast (not sugary cereal that will leave you tired by the middle of the morning). An egg or a milkshake with yogurt and fresh fruit will give you lasting energy. Also, wear comfortable clothes, maybe your lucky shirt or your favorite color on test day. It can't hurt, and it may even keep you relax.

Be prepared. Do practice questions and learn about how standardized tests are organized. Books like this one will help you know what to expect when you take a standardized test.

When you are taking the test, follow the directions. It is important to listen carefully to the directions your teacher gives and to read the written instructions carefully. Words like *not, none, rarely, never,* and *always* are very important in test directions and questions. You may want to circle words like these.

Look at each page carefully before you start answering. In school you usually read a passage and then answer questions about it. But when you take a test, it's helpful to follow a different order.

If you are taking a Reading test, first read the directions. Then read the *questions* before you read the passage. This way you will know exactly what kind of information to look for as you read. Next, read the passage carefully. Finally, answer the questions.

On math and science tests, look at the labels on graphs and charts. Think about what each graph or chart shows. Questions often will ask you to draw conclusions about the information.

Manage your time. *Time management* means using your time wisely on a test so that you can finish as much of it as possible and do your best. Look over the test or the parts that you are allowed to do at one time. Sometimes you may want to do the easier parts first. This way, if you run out of time before you finish, you will have completed a good chunk of the work.

For tests that have a time limit, notice what time it is when the test begins and figure out when you need to stop. Check a few times as you work through the test to be sure you are making good progress and not spending too much time on any particular section.

You don't have to keep up with everyone else. You may notice other students in the class finishing before you do. Don't worry about this. Everyone works at a different pace. Just keep going, trying not to spend too long on any one question.

Fill in answer circles properly. Even if you know every answer on a test, you won't do well unless you fill in the circle next to the correct answer.

Fill in the entire circle, but don't spend too much time making it perfect. Make your mark dark, but not so dark that it goes through the paper! And be sure you only choose one answer for each question, even if you are not sure. If you choose two answers, both will be marked as wrong.

It's usually not a good idea to change your answers. Usually your first choice is the right one. Unless you realize that you misread the question, the directions, or some facts in a passage, it's usually safer to stay with your first answer. If you are pretty sure it's wrong, of course, go ahead and change it. Make sure you completely erase the first choice and neatly fill in your new choice.

Use context clues to figure out tough questions. If you come across a word or idea you don't understand, use context clues—the words in the sentences nearby— to help you figure out its meaning.

Sometimes it's good to guess. Should you guess when you don't know an answer on a test? That depends. If your teacher has made the test, usually you will score better if you answer as many questions as possible, even if you don't really know the answers.

On standardized tests, here's what to do to score your best. For each question, most of these tests let you choose from four or five answer choices. If you decide that a couple of answers are clearly wrong but you're still not sure about the answer, go ahead and make your best guess. If you can't narrow down the choices at all, then you may be better off skipping the question. Tests like these take away extra points for wrong answers, so it's better to leave them blank. Be sure you skip over the answer space for these questions on the answer sheet, though, so you don't fill in the wrong spaces.

Sometimes you should skip a question and come back to it. On many tests, you will score better if you answer more questions. This means that you should not spend too much time on any single question. Sometimes it gets tricky, though, keeping track of questions you skipped on your answer sheet.

If you want to skip a question because you don't know the answer, put a very light pencil mark next to the question in the test booklet. Try to choose an answer, even if you're not sure of it. Fill in the answer lightly on the answer sheet.

Check your work. On a standardized test, you can't go ahead or skip back to another section of the test. But you may go back and review your answers on the section you just worked on if you have extra time.

First, scan your answer sheet. Make sure that you answered every question you could. Also, if you are using a bubble-type answer sheet, make sure that you filled in only one bubble for each question. Erase any extra marks on the page.

Finally—avoid test anxiety! If you get nervous about tests, don't worry. *Test anxiety* happens to lots of good students. Being a little nervous actually sharpens your mind. But if you get very nervous about tests, take a few minutes to relax the night before or the day of the test. One good way to relax is to get some exercise, even if you just have time to stretch, shake out your fingers, and wiggle your toes. If you can't move around, it helps just to take a few slow, deep breaths and picture yourself doing a great job!

Terms to Know

Here's a list of terms that are good to know when taking standardized tests. Don't be worried if you see something new. You may not have learned it in school yet.

acute angle: an angle of less than 90°

adjective: a word that describes a noun (*yellow duckling*, *new bicycle*)

adverb: a word that describes a verb (*ran fast*, *laughing heartily*)

analogy: a comparison of the relationship between two or more otherwise unrelated things (*Carrot is to vegetable as banana is to fruit.*)

angle: the figure formed by two lines that start at the same point, usually shown in degrees

antonyms: words with opposite meanings (*big and small, young and old*)

area: the amount of space inside a flat shape, expressed in square units

article: a word such as *a*, *an*, or *the* that goes in front of a noun (*the chicken, an apple*)

cause/effect: the reason that something happens

character: a person in a story, book, movie, play, or TV show

compare/contrast: to tell what is alike and different about two or more things

compass rose: the symbol on a map that shows where North, South, East, and West are

conclusion: a logical decision you can make based on information from a reading selection or science experiment

congruent: equal in size or shape

context clues: language and details in a piece of writing that can help you figure out difficult words and ideas

denominator: in a fraction, the number under the line, shows how many equal parts a whole has been divided into ($\frac{1}{2}$, $\frac{6}{7}$)

direct object: in a sentence, the person or thing that receives the action of a verb (*John hit the ball hard.*)

equation: in math, a statement where one set of numbers or values is equal to another set ($6 + 6 = 12$, $4 \times 5 = 20$)

factor: a whole number that can be divided exactly into another whole number (*1, 2, 3, 4, and 6 are all factors of 12.*)

genre: a category of literature that contains writing with common features (*drama, fiction, nonfiction, poetry*)

hypothesis: in science, the possible answer to a question; most science experiments begin with a hypothesis

indirect object: in a sentence, the noun or pronoun that tells to or for whom the action of the verb is done (*Louise gave a flower to her sister.*)

infer: to make an educated guess about a piece of writing, based on information contained in the selection and what you already know

main idea: the most important idea or message in a writing selection

map legend: the part of a map showing symbols that represent natural or human-made objects

noun: a person, place, or thing (*president, underground, train*)

numerator: in a fraction, the number above the line, shows how many equal parts are to be taken from the denominator ($\frac{3}{4}$, $\frac{1}{5}$)

operation: in math, tells what must be done to numbers in an equation (such as add, subtract, multiply, or divide)

parallel: lines or rays that, if extended, could never intersect

percent: fraction of a whole that has been divided into 100 parts, usually expressed with % sign ($\frac{5}{100} = 5\%$)

perimeter: distance around an object or shape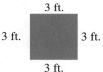

perpendicular: lines or rays that intersect to form a 90° (right) angle

predicate: in a sentence, the word or words that tell what the subject does, did, or has (*The fuzzy kitten had black spots on its belly.*)

predict: in science or reading, to use given information to decide what will happen

prefixes/suffixes: letters added to the beginning or end of a word to change its meaning (*reorganize, hopeless*)

preposition: a word that shows the relationship between a noun or pronoun and other words in a phrase or sentence (*We sat by the fire. She walked through the door.*)

probability: the likelihood that something will happen, often shown with numbers

pronoun: a word that is used in place of a noun (*She gave the present to them.*)

ratio: a comparison of two quantities, often shown as a fraction (*The ratio of boys to girls in the class is 2 to 1, or 2/1.*)

sequence: the order in which events happen or in which items can be placed in a pattern

subject: in a sentence, the word or words that tells who or what the sentence is about (*Uncle Robert baked the cake. Everyone at the party ate it.*)

summary: a restatement of important ideas from a selection in the writer's own words

synonyms: words with the same, or almost the same, meaning (*delicious and tasty, funny and comical*)

symmetry: in math and science, two or more sides or faces of an object that are mirror images of one another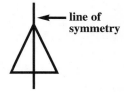

Venn diagram: two or more overlapping circles used to compare and contrast two or more things

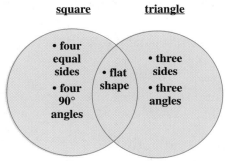

verb: a word that describes an action or state of being (*He watched the fireworks.*)

writing prompt: on a test, a question or statement that you must respond to in writing

Skills Checklist

Which subjects do you need more practice in? Use the following checklist to find out. Put a check mark next to each statement that is true for you. Then use the unchecked statements to figure out which skills you need to review.

Keep in mind that if you are using these checklists in the middle of the school year, you may not have learned some skills yet. Talk to your teacher or a parent if you need help with a new skill.

Reading

☐ I can use context clues to figure out tough words.

☐ I know what synonyms are and how to use them.

☐ I can find words with opposite meanings.

☐ I can find the main idea or theme of a passage.

☐ I can figure out the author's purpose for writing a passage.

Language Arts

I can identify the different parts of speech.

☐ common and proper nouns

☐ plural nouns

☐ possessive nouns

☐ pronouns

☐ verbs

☐ adjectives

☐ adverbs

☐ articles

☐ I can tell the difference between a complete and an incomplete sentence.

Writing

Before I write

☐ I think about my audience.

☐ I think about my purpose for writing (to persuade, inform, or entertain).

When I write a draft

☐ I use paragraphs that have a main idea and supporting details.

☐ I use words and actions that tell about my characters.

☐ I include details about the setting.

☐ I use reference materials (encyclopedias, dictionaries, the Internet) to find information.

As I revise my work

☐ I check for spelling, capitalization, punctuation, and grammar mistakes.

☐ I take out parts that aren't necessary.

☐ I add words and sentences to make my work more interesting.

☐ I neatly write or type my final copy.

☐ I include my name and a title on the finished work.

Mathematics

Addition and Subtraction

 I know addition and subtraction facts to 18.

☐ I can regroup when adding or subtracting two- or three-digit numbers.

Multiplication and Division

☐ I practice my multiplication and division facts so I can do them quickly.

☐ I can multiply by one-digit numbers.

 I can regroup when multiplying with one-, two-, and three-digit numbers.

☐ I can divide by one-digit numbers with and without remainders.

Measurement

I know my standard units of measure for

 length (inch, foot, yard, mile).

☐ weight (ounce, pound).

☐ capacity (cup, pint, quart, gallon).

☐ time (seconds, minutes, hours).

I know my metric units of measure for

 length (centimeter, decimeter, meter, kilometer).

 mass (gram, kilogram).

 capacity (liter).

 I can solve simple problems with units of time, length, weight/mass, and capacity.

Fractions and Decimals

 I can name parts of a whole (one-half, one-third, one-quarter).

 I can compare like and unlike fractions.

I can read mixed numbers.

I can read decimals to the tenths and hundredths places.

Geometry

For simple shapes, I can

 calculate perimeter and area.

 find lines of symmetry.

Problem Solving

 When I do number problems, I read the directions carefully.

 When I do word problems, I read the problem carefully.

I look for words that tell the operation I must use to solve the problem.

I label my answer with units when necessary.

I use different strategies to solve different kinds of problems:

 I estimate.

 I make pictures, diagrams, and charts.

I look for patterns.

Preparing All Year Round

Believe it or not, knowing how to study and manage your time is a skill you will use for the rest of your life. There are helpful strategies that you can use to be more successful in school. The following is a list of tips to keep in mind as you study for tests and school assignments.

Get organized. To make it easy to get your homework done, set up a place in which to do it each day. Choose a location where you can give the work your full attention. Find a corner of your room, the kitchen, or another quiet place where you won't be interrupted. Put all the tools you'll need in that area. Set aside a drawer or basket for school supplies. That way you won't have to go hunting each time you need a sharp pencil! Here are some things you may want to keep in your study corner for homework and school projects:

- pencils and pens
- pencil sharpener
- notebook paper
- tape
- glue
- scissors
- stapler
- crayons, markers, colored pencils
- construction paper, printer paper
- dictionary

Schedule your assignments. The best way to keep track of homework and special projects is by planning and managing your time. Keep a schedule of homework assignments and other events to help you get organized. Make your own or make a copy of the Homework Log and Weekly Schedule provided on pages 22–23 of this book for each week you're in school.

Record your homework assignments on the log as completely as you can. Enter the book, page number, and exercise number of each assignment. Enter dates of tests as soon as you know them so that you can begin to study ahead of time. Study a section of the material each day. Then review all of it the day before the test.

Also make notes to help you remember special events and materials such as permission slips you need to return. List after-school activities so you can plan your homework and study time around them. Remember to record fun activities on your log, too. You don't want to forget that party you've been invited to or even just time you'd like to spend hanging out or studying with friends.

Do your homework right away. Set aside a special time every day after school to do your homework. You may want to take a break when you first get home, but give yourself plenty of time to do your homework, too. That way you won't get interrupted by dinner or get too tired to finish.

If you are bored or confused by an assignment and you really don't want to do it, promise yourself a little reward, perhaps a snack or 15 minutes of playing ball after you've really worked hard for 45 minutes or so. Then go back to work for a while if you need to, and take another break later.

Get help if you need it. If you need help, just ask. Call a friend or ask a family member for help. If these people can't help you, be sure to ask your teacher the next day about any work you didn't understand.

Use a computer. If you have one available, a computer can be a great tool for doing homework. Typing your homework on the computer lets you hand in neat papers, check your spelling easily, and look up the definitions of words you aren't sure about. If you have an Internet connection, you can also do research without leaving home.

Before you go online, talk with your family about ways to stay safe. Be sure never to give out personal information (your name, age, address, or phone number) without permission.

Practice, practice, practice! The best way to improve your skills in specific subject areas is through lots of practice. If you have trouble in a school subject such as math, science, social studies, language arts, or reading, doing some extra activities or projects can give you just the boost you need.

Homework Log
and Weekly Schedule

	Monday	Tuesday	Wednesday
MATH			
SOCIAL STUDIES			
SCIENCE			
READING			
LANGUAGE ARTS			
OTHER			

for the week of _____

Thursday	Friday	Saturday / Sunday	
			MATH
			SOCIAL STUDIES
			SCIENCE
			READING
			LANGUAGE ARTS
			OTHER

What's Ahead in This Book?

As you know, you will have to take many tests while in school. But there is no reason to be nervous about taking standardized tests. You can prepare for them by doing your best in school all year. You can also learn about the types of questions you'll see on standardized tests and helpful strategies for answering the questions. That's what this book is all about. It has been developed especially to help you and other third graders know what to expect—and what to do—on test day.

The first section will introduce you to the different kinds of questions found on most standardized tests. Multiple choice, short answer, matching, and other types of questions will be explained in detail. You'll get tips for answering each type. Then you'll be given sample questions to work through so you can practice your skills.

Next, you'll find sections on these major school subjects: reading, language arts, math, social studies (sometimes called citizenship), and science. You'll discover traps to watch for in each subject area and tricks you can use to make answering the questions easier. And there are plenty of practice questions provided to sharpen your skills even more.

Finally, you'll find two sections of questions. One is called Practice Test and the other is called Final Test. The questions are designed to look just like the ones you'll be given in school on a real standardized test. An answer key is at the back of the book so you can check your own answers. Once you check your answers, you can see in which subject areas you need more practice.

So good luck—test success is just around the corner!

Multiple Choice Questions

You have probably seen multiple choice questions before. They are the most common type of question used on standardized tests. To answer a multiple choice question, you must choose one answer from a number of choices.

EXAMPLE   **Another word for <u>unsafe</u> is _____.**

   Ⓐ safe

   Ⓑ dangerous

   Ⓒ unkind

   Ⓓ careful

Sometimes you will know the answer right away. Other times you won't. To answer multiple choice questions on a test, do the following:

- Read the directions carefully. If you're not sure what you're supposed to do, you might make a lot of mistakes.
- First answer any easy questions whose answers you are sure you know.
- When you come to a harder question, circle the question number. You can come back to this question after you have finished all the easier ones.
- When you're ready to answer a hard question, throw out answers that you know are wrong. You can do this by making an X after each choice you know is not correct. The last choice left is probably the correct one.

Testing It Out

Now look at the sample question more closely.

Think: I know that *safe* is the opposite of *unsafe*, so **A** cannot be the correct answer. I think that *cautious* is like being *careful*, so **D** is probably not the right answer.

Now I have to choose between **C** and **B**. Let's see: *unkind* has the word *kind* in it, and **un** usually means *not*, so I think that *unkind* means *not kind*. However, something that is *dangerous* is definitely not safe. So **B** must be the correct choice.

Multiple Choice Practice

Directions: For questions 1–4, find the word that means the same or nearly the same as the underlined word. Fill in the circle next to the correct answer.

1 **gobble the popcorn**

Ⓐ scramble

Ⓑ guzzle

Ⓒ eat

Ⓓ drink

2 **under the table**

Ⓕ beneath

Ⓖ along

Ⓗ above

Ⓙ inside

3 **delicious cookies**

Ⓐ bad

Ⓑ tasty

Ⓒ comfortable

Ⓓ valuable

4 **water pitcher**

Ⓕ picture   Ⓗ mug

Ⓖ liquid   Ⓙ jug

Directions: Read the story below and answer questions 5–7.

On Sunday we ate breakfast in a restaurant. Dad ordered fried eggs, bacon, pancakes, and coffee. I ordered waffles with strawberries and a glass of orange juice. Mom wasn't very hungry, so she just had toast and coffee. After breakfast we took a walk in the park.

5 **What did the family do before breakfast?**

Ⓐ took a walk on the beach

Ⓑ took a walk in the park

Ⓒ walked to the restaurant

Ⓓ does not tell

6 **What did Mom and Dad drink?**

Ⓕ strawberry juice

Ⓖ coffee

Ⓗ orange juice

Ⓙ different drinks

7 **What did the author eat?**

Ⓐ eggs

Ⓑ toast

Ⓒ waffles with strawberries

Ⓓ does not tell

Fill-in-the-Blank Questions

On some tests, you will be given multiple choice questions where you must fill in something that's missing from a phrase, sentence, equation, or passage. These are called "fill-in-the-blank" questions.

EXAMPLE **Tricia felt _____ that Robyn could not come to her party.**

Ⓐ disturbed

Ⓑ distorted

Ⓒ dissolved

Ⓓ disappointed

To answer fill-in-the-blank questions:

- First read the item with a blank that needs to be filled.
- See if you can think of the answer even before you look at your choices.
- Even if the answer you first thought of is one of the choices, be sure to check the other choices. There may be an even better answer.
- For harder questions, try to fit every answer choice into the blank. Underline clue words that may help you find the correct answer. Write an **X** after answers that do not fit. Choose the answer that does fit.

Testing It Out

Now look at the sample question above more closely.

Think: Choice **A** says, "Tricia felt *disturbed* that Robyn could not come to her party." I guess someone *might* feel disturbed if a friend could not come to her party.

Choice **B** says, "Tricia felt *dissolved* that Robyn could not come to her party." That sounds silly—people don't feel dissolved. That choice is wrong.

Choice **C** says, "Tricia felt *distorted* that Robyn could not come to her party." I have never heard of anyone feeling distorted. That choice must be wrong, too.

Choice **D** says, "Tricia felt *disappointed* that Robyn could not come to her party." This is how I would feel if a friend could not come to my party. I'll choose **D**.

Fill-in-the-Blank Practice

Directions: Find the word that best completes each sentence.
Fill in the circle next to each correct answer.

1 Tricia's party had a space travel _____.

Ⓐ them   Ⓒ thread

Ⓑ theme   Ⓓ themselves

2 Her dad made space _____ out of balloons.

Ⓕ allies   Ⓗ aliens

Ⓖ alienate   Ⓙ alias

3 He made a space _____ for every party guest.

Ⓐ hem   Ⓒ helm

Ⓑ help   Ⓓ helmet

4 He ran the vacuum _____ to make a spaceship engine sound.

Ⓕ cleaner   Ⓗ cleaning

Ⓖ cleanser   Ⓙ cleans

5 Dad made a control _____ with lots of buttons and levers.

Ⓐ pane   Ⓒ paddle

Ⓑ panel   Ⓓ petal

6 He typed on his computer _____, pretending to run the spaceship.

Ⓕ key   Ⓗ keyboard

Ⓖ keying   Ⓙ keen

7 Later, everyone watched _____ of a space movie.

Ⓐ a radio   Ⓒ a cell phone

Ⓑ an audio tape   Ⓓ a video tape

8 Tricia's cake was _____ to look like the surface of the moon.

Ⓕ decorating   Ⓗ decorated

Ⓖ decorates   Ⓙ decorate

9 It had mountains and _____ made out of frosting.

Ⓐ graders   Ⓒ crates

Ⓑ craters   Ⓓ graters

10 Tricia _____ many wonderful gifts.

Ⓕ rescued   Ⓗ returned

Ⓖ received   Ⓙ retained

True/False Questions

A true/false question asks you to read a statement and decide if it is right (true) or wrong (false). Sometimes you will be asked to write **T** for true or **F** for false. Most of the time you must fill in a bubble next to the correct answer.

EXAMPLE   **Milk is the only ingredient in yogurt.**

    Ⓐ   true

    Ⓑ   false

To answer true/false questions on a test, think about the following:

- True/false sections contain more questions than other sections of a test. If there is a time limit on the test, you may need to go a little more quickly than usual. Do not spend too much time on any one question.
- First answer all of the easy questions. Circle the numbers next to harder ones and come back to them later.
- If you have time left after completing all the questions, quickly double-check your answers.
- True/false questions with words like *always, never, none, only,* and *every* are usually false. This is because they limit a statement so much.

Remember

True/false questions with words like *always, never, none, only* and *every* are usually false.

Testing It Out

Now look at the sample question more closely.

Think: I see the word *only* in this statement. I know that milk is the main ingredient in yogurt—it tastes a lot like milk. But some kinds of yogurt have fruit in them, and I think they must have sugar, too. I will mark this answer **B** for false.

True/False Questions

Directions: Decide if each statement is true or false.
Fill in the circle next to the correct answer.

1 Milk, cheese, and yogurt are all dairy products.

Ⓐ true   Ⓑ false

2 Wheat is not a dairy product.

Ⓐ true   Ⓑ false

3 Every child loves chocolate ice cream.

Ⓐ true   Ⓑ false

4 Adults and children like chocolate ice cream better than vanilla.

Ⓐ true   Ⓑ false

5 Nonfat milk is less fattening than whole milk.

Ⓐ true   Ⓑ false

6 All yogurt brands contain fruit.

Ⓐ true   Ⓑ false

7 There are 50 states in the U.S.A.

Ⓐ true   Ⓑ false

8 Washington, D.C. is a city.

Ⓐ true   Ⓑ false

9 Washington is a state.

Ⓐ true   Ⓑ false

10 New York City is the capital of the United States.

Ⓐ true   Ⓑ false

11 Massachusetts is north of Virginia.

Ⓐ true   Ⓑ false

12 Hawaii is east of California.

Ⓐ true   Ⓑ false

13 People drink only cow's milk.

Ⓐ true   Ⓑ false

14 Wyoming is south of Montana.

Ⓐ true   Ⓑ false

Matching Questions

Matching questions ask you to find pairs of words or phrases that go together. The choices are often shown in columns.

EXAMPLE   **Match items that mean the same, or almost the same, thing.**

1 **happy**	Ⓐ mournful	1	Ⓐ Ⓑ Ⓒ Ⓓ
2 **angry**	Ⓑ flabbergasted	2	Ⓐ Ⓑ Ⓒ Ⓓ
3 **surprised**	Ⓒ joyful	3	Ⓐ Ⓑ Ⓒ Ⓓ
4 **sad**	Ⓓ furious	4	Ⓐ Ⓑ Ⓒ Ⓓ

When answering matching questions on tests, there are some simple guidelines you can use:

- When you first look at a matching question, you will probably be able to spot some of the matches right away. So match the easiest choices first.
- If you come to a word you don't know, look for prefixes, suffixes, or root words to help figure out its meaning.
- Work down one column at a time. It is confusing to switch back and forth.

Testing It Out

Now look at the sample question more closely.

Think: What's a word from the second column that goes with *happy*? *Joyful* has the word *joy* in it, which is like happiness, so the answer to **1** must be **C.**

I know that *furious* is another word for *angry*, so the answer to 2 is **D.**

I'm not sure which of the remaining choices means the same as *surprised*, so I'll come back to that one.

For *sad*, I'm not sure what the best match is; however, I see that *mournful* has the word *mourn* in it, and people mourn when someone dies. Since people mourn when someone dies and they are also sad, then I'll choose **A** as the match for *sad*.

Going back to *surprised*, the only remaining choice is **B**, *flabbergasted*. That must be the correct choice, since I am fairly certain of my other answers.

Matching Practice

Directions: For numbers 1–16, match words or phrases with the same, or almost the same, meanings.

1	baby	A	adolescent	1	Ⓐ Ⓑ Ⓒ Ⓓ
2	grown-up	B	infant	2	Ⓐ Ⓑ Ⓒ Ⓓ
3	teenager	C	toddler	3	Ⓐ Ⓑ Ⓒ Ⓓ
4	small child	D	adult	4	Ⓐ Ⓑ Ⓒ Ⓓ

5	couch	F	cabinet	5	Ⓕ Ⓖ Ⓗ Ⓙ
6	dresser	G	bureau	6	Ⓕ Ⓖ Ⓗ Ⓙ
7	cupboard	H	drapes	7	Ⓕ Ⓖ Ⓗ Ⓙ
8	curtains	J	sofa	8	Ⓕ Ⓖ Ⓗ Ⓙ

9	hungry	A	exhausted	9	Ⓐ Ⓑ Ⓒ Ⓓ
10	sleepy	B	thrilled	10	Ⓐ Ⓑ Ⓒ Ⓓ
11	excited	C	ravenous	11	Ⓐ Ⓑ Ⓒ Ⓓ
12	interested	D	intrigued	12	Ⓐ Ⓑ Ⓒ Ⓓ

13	look at	F	sprint	13	Ⓕ Ⓖ Ⓗ Ⓙ
14	walk	G	stroll	14	Ⓕ Ⓖ Ⓗ Ⓙ
15	run	H	view	15	Ⓕ Ⓖ Ⓗ Ⓙ
16	eat	J	gobble	16	Ⓕ Ⓖ Ⓗ Ⓙ

Analogy Questions

Analogies are a special kind of question. In an analogy question, you are asked to figure out the relationship between two things. Then you must complete another pair with the same relationship.

EXAMPLE **Carrot is to vegetable as orange is to _____.**

   Ⓐ celery   Ⓒ apple

   Ⓑ sweet   Ⓓ fruit

Analogies usually have two pairs of items. In the question above the two pairs are carrot/vegetable and orange/_____. To answer analogy questions on standardized tests, do the following:

- Find the missing item that completes the second pair. To do this, you must figure out how the first pair of items relate to each other. Try to form a sentence that explains how they are related.
- Next, use your sentence to figure out the missing word in the second pair of items.
- For more difficult analogies, try each answer choice in the sentence you formed. Choose the answer that fits best.

Testing It Out

Now look at the sample question more closely.

Think: How are carrots and vegetables related? A carrot is a kind of vegetable. So if I use the word *orange* in this sentence, I'd say, an *orange* is a kind of _____.

Choice **A** is *celery*. If I use *celery* to complete the sentence, I end up with *An orange is a kind of celery*. I think that celery is a vegetable. That choice must be wrong.

Choice **B** is *sweet*. *An orange is a kind of sweet*. No, that's not right, either. Oranges are sweet, but they're not a kind of sweet.

Choice **C** is *apple*. *An orange is a kind of apple*. I know that that answer is wrong because that sentence makes no sense.

Choice **D** would be *An orange is a kind of fruit*. Yes, I think that's true. So the answer must be **D**.

Analogy Practice

Directions: Find the word that best completes each analogy. Fill in the circle next to the correct answer.

1 **Boy** is to **girl** as **man** is to _____.

Ⓐ teenager   Ⓒ woman

Ⓑ male   Ⓓ older

2 **Tiny** is to **enormous** as **mournful** is to _____.

Ⓕ sad   Ⓗ huge

Ⓖ joyful   Ⓙ empty

3 **Q** is to **letter** as **15** is to _____.

Ⓐ quail   Ⓒ K

Ⓑ thirty   Ⓓ number

4 **Circus** is to **clown** as **ballet** is to _____.

Ⓕ magician   Ⓗ dancer

Ⓖ dance   Ⓙ performance

5 **blueberry** is to **raspberry** as **pecan** is to _____.

Ⓐ pie   Ⓒ blackberry

Ⓑ walnut   Ⓓ nut

6 **Beef** is to **meat** as **rice** is to _____.

Ⓕ cakes   Ⓗ wheat

Ⓖ pork   Ⓙ grain

7 **Thirteen** is to **teenager** as **forty** is to _____.

Ⓐ adult   Ⓒ toddler

Ⓑ fifteen   Ⓓ four

8 **Mean** is to **nasty** as **nice** is to _____.

Ⓕ kind   Ⓗ angry

Ⓖ rough   Ⓙ sad

9 **Bird** is to **cage** as **fish** is to _____.

Ⓐ ocean   Ⓒ water

Ⓑ tank   Ⓓ stream

10 **Teller** is to **bank** as **cashier** is to _____.

Ⓕ grocery store   Ⓗ money

Ⓖ grocery cart   Ⓙ groceries

Short Answer Questions

Some test questions don't give you answers to choose from; instead, you must write short answers in your own words. These are called "short answer" or "open response" questions. For example:

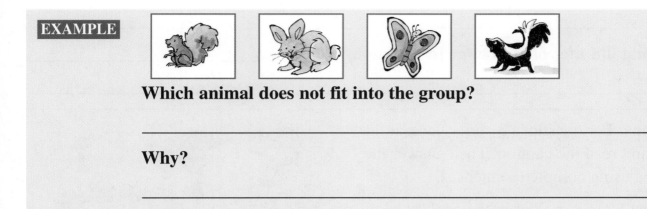

EXAMPLE

Which animal does not fit into the group?

_____

Why?

_____

When you must write short answers to questions on a standardized test:

- Make sure to respond directly to the question that is being asked.
- Your response should be short but complete. Don't waste time including unnecessary information. On the other hand, make sure to answer the entire question, not just a part of it.
- Write in complete sentences unless the directions say you don't have to.
- Double-check your answers for spelling, punctuation, and grammar mistakes.

Testing It Out

Now look at the sample question more closely.

Think: Squirrels, rabbits, and skunks are all mammals. They have fur and four legs. But butterflies are insects. So *butterfly* must be the animal that does not fit.

Since there are no instructions about what to write for each answer, I should use complete sentences. So I'll write:

Which animal does not fit into the group?

The butterfly does not fit into the group.

Why?

A butterfly is an insect. All the other animals shown are mammals.

Short Answer Practice

Directions: For questions 1 and 2, write short answers using complete sentences.

1 **Who did the colonies fight against in the Revolutionary War?** _____

_____

2 **What did the colonies hope to accomplish?**_____

_____

Directions: For questions 3 and 4, look at the picture and read the caption. Then answer the questions using complete sentences.

Hot air balloons can float in the cooler air around them. When the hot air is released from the balloons, they come back to Earth's surface.

3 **Why does hot air float?** _____

_____

4 **What force brings the balloon to Earth after the hot air is let out?**

_____

Directions: Read the following passage and answer the questions below.

The sound of the alarm filled Captain Mack's ears. "Fire in the engine room," announced the computer, calmly. The crew looked at Mack with questions in their eyes. The spacecraft was far from Earth and they would have to handle any problems themselves. Mack quickly closed off the oxygen to the engine room to help put out the fire. Then he sent crew members back to clean up the mess. Soon the spacecraft was safe and on its way to Mars.

5 **What do you think the crew members were feeling when the alarm first sounded?**

_____

6 **What kind of leader do you think Captain Mack was? Why?** _____

_____

Reading

Many standardized tests have sections called "Reading" or "Reading Comprehension." Reading Comprehension questions test your ability to read for detail, find meaning in a sentence or passage, and use context clues to figure out words or ideas you don't understand.

The following is a list of topics covered on Reading Comprehension tests. Look at the tips and examples that go with each topic.

Word Meaning
Word meaning questions test your vocabulary and your ability to figure out unfamiliar words. When answering questions about word meaning:

• Look at words carefully and see if you can find prefixes, suffixes, or root words that give clues to their meaning. If you look at the underlined word below, *unusual*, you can see it contains the prefix **un** (which means not) and a root word, *usual* (common or ordinary). So you can guess that the word means something like "not common" or "not ordinary."

We saw some <u>unusual</u> animals at the zoo.

• For clues to a more difficult word's meaning, look at the other words in the sentence or passage. If you look at the example below, for instance, you can tell by the use of words like *detective* and

mystery that solved means "found the answer to" or "explained."

The detective <u>solved</u> the mystery of the missing jewels.

Characterization
What characters say, do, and feel is an important part of many reading passages. Often you can tell what a character is feeling by what he or she says or does.

When Joey heard the winning score, he jumped up and cheered.

Cause and Effect
Look for **cause and effect** when you read. A **cause** is an event that makes another event happen. The **effect** is the event that is caused.

• Words like *before, after*, and *because* can provide clues to cause and effect.

Sheila was mad at her sister because she had borrowed her shirt without asking.

In this sentence, Sheila's sister borrowing a shirt is the cause and Sheila being mad is the effect.

Sequence
The **sequence of events** is the order in which events take place in a story or article. Sometimes events are listed in sequence. Other times, they aren't.

Reading Practice

Directions: Read the passage and then answer the questions. Fill in the circle next to each answer.

Alanna loved to run. She ran to school and she ran home from school. She ran to her friends' houses and to the library. Most of the time she ran upstairs and downstairs in her family's house. "Are you sure you're not part cheetah?" her mother joked as Alanna whizzed past her on her way to the basement. "I think I'll train for the marathon this summer to raise money for the homeless shelter," Alanna told her mother. She knew the winner would get a trophy and $1000 to donate to the shelter.

Alanna began to train seriously for the marathon. She bought a new pair of running shoes. She ran on the school track and on the sidewalks of her community. After about a month, she began to have pain in her knees. The pain increased, but she kept running. Soon the pain got so bad her mother took her the doctor. "You have runner's knees," the doctor said. "You run too much without warming up. You'll have to do some exercises to strengthen your knees."

Alanna had to slow down for a week or so. As she exercised, her pain decreased. Soon she was running as before. At the end of August she ran the marathon and won. All her friends cheered as she broke the tape.

1 **What word best describes Alanna?**

Ⓐ clever

Ⓑ athletic

Ⓒ musical

Ⓓ stubborn

2 **Which pair of words from the story mean the opposite of one another?**

Ⓕ increased/decreased

Ⓖ cheetah/runner

Ⓗ winner/friend

Ⓙ pain/exercise

3 **What is a <u>marathon</u>?**

Ⓐ a kind of race

Ⓑ a kind of runner

Ⓒ a kind of running shoe

Ⓓ a kind of exercise

4 **What was the cause of Alanna's pain?**

Ⓕ running without the proper shoes

Ⓖ running on the sidewalk

Ⓗ running without warming up

Ⓙ running around her house

Writing

Many tests will ask you to respond to a writing prompt. When responding to a writing prompt, follow these guidelines:

EXAMPLE

Do you think Little Red Riding Hood was a smart girl? Write a paragraph explaining your answer.

The following is a list of guidelines to use when responding to a writing prompt.

Reading the Prompt

- Read the instructions carefully. Sometimes you will be given a choice of questions or topics to write about. You don't want to end up responding to more questions than you need to.
- Read the prompt twice to be sure you understand it. Remember, there is no one right response to a writing prompt.

Prewriting

- Before you write your answer, jot down some details to include.
- You may find it helpful to use a chart, web, illustration, or outline to help you organize the information you want to include in your response.

A web is a way of organizing your thoughts. If you were writing about Little Red Riding Hood, your web might look like this:

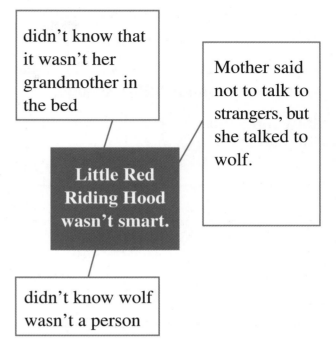

Drafting

- Begin your answer with a **topic sentence** that answers the question and gives the main idea.
- Write **supporting sentences** that give details and tell more about the main idea.
- If you are allowed, skip lines as you write. That way you'll have space to correct your mistakes once you're done writing.

Proofreading

- Make sure to proofread your draft for missing words, grammar, punctuation, capitalization, indentation, and spelling. Correct your mistakes.

Writing Practice

Directions: Write a paragraph to answer one of the questions below.

Who is the scariest villain you have read about or seen in a movie? Explain what you think is scary about this character.

Many fairy tales have wolves for villains. Do you think this is fair to real-life wolves? Explain your answer.

Language Arts

Mechanics and Expression

Standardized tests usually include questions about spelling, grammar, punctuation, and capitalization. These questions are often grouped together in sections called "Language Mechanics and Expression" or "Language Arts."

The following is a list of the different topics included under Language Mechanics and Expression. Look at the tips and examples that go with each topic.

Grammar

Grammar is the set of rules that helps you write good, clear sentences. Whether you are answering a multiple choice question, writing a short answer, or responding to a writing prompt, you should:

- Be sure the subject and verb of each sentence agree with each other.

> Sam **brushes** his dog.
> [singular subject and verb]
>
> Sam and Gina **brush** their dog.
> [plural subject and verb]

- Remember how to use different parts of speech such as nouns, verbs, adjectives, adverbs, and pronouns.

> Lila ate quickly. She was hungry.
> [noun-verb-adverb-pronoun-verb-adjective]

Capitalization

You may be asked to identify words that should be capitalized and words that shouldn't. Remember:

- always capitalize the first word in a sentence.
- always capitalize the names of people, places, and other proper nouns.

> The **R**amirez family visited the **G**rand **C**anyon in **J**uly.
>
> **T**hey sent postcards to the **S**osas and the **M**orleys.

Punctuation

You will probably be given multiple choice questions about punctuation, but you will also be required to use punctuation marks when you write answers in your own words.

- Make sure to check punctuation at the end of sentences *and* within them.

> Did you pack the food**?**
> *[question mark]*
>
> I think I put it in the car**.**
> *[period]*
>
> Wait, I left the food in the garage**!**
> *[comma, exclamation point]*
>
> We can buy fruit, sandwiches, and pop at the market. *[commas]*

Language Arts

Spelling

You may be asked to pick out misspelled words or choose the correct spelling of a word that is already misspelled. You should also check your own spelling when you write.

> The Grand Canyon is 500 **mils** from our **hom**.
> *[incorrect]*
>
> The Grand Canyon is 500 **miles** from our **home**.
> *[correct]*

Sentence Structure

Remember to use complete sentences whenever you write a short answer or paragraph. To tell if a sentence is complete:

- make sure the sentence has a subject and a verb.
- make sure the sentence starts with a capital letter and ends with the correct punctuation mark.

> barked at us as we drove by
> *[fragment]*
>
> The dog barked at us as we drove by.
> *[complete sentence]*

Also keep in mind:

- avoid beginning sentences with *And*.
- you can often make two sentences more interesting by combining them into one. However, you should be careful not to change the sentences' meaning.

> Jed went to the movie. Alice went to the movie. Sandy stayed home.
>
> Jed and Alice went to the movie, but Sandy stayed home.
> *[combined]*

Remember

- ¥ Make sure each sentence has a subject and predicate.
- ¥ Start each sentence with a capital letter.
- ¥ End each sentence with the correct punctuation mark.

Language Arts Practice

Directions: Choose the punctuation that is missing from numbers 1–4.

1 **Oh no, we lost the game again**

     "   none   !   .

    Ⓐ   Ⓑ   Ⓒ   Ⓓ

2 **Is that your cousin James**

     .   ,   !   ?

    Ⓕ   Ⓖ   Ⓗ   Ⓙ

3 **The Harrises have dogs cats and horses.**

     .   ,   !   ?

    Ⓐ   Ⓑ   Ⓒ   Ⓓ

4 **I can't believe you forgot to buy milk again, my sister exclaimed.**

     ,   !   " "   ?

    Ⓕ   Ⓖ   Ⓗ   Ⓙ

Directions: For numbers 5–7, choose the correct verb to complete each sentence.

5 **Jed _____ soccer every Saturday.**

Ⓐ playing   Ⓒ play

Ⓑ plays   Ⓓ are playing

6 **The cat ____ from the dog.**

Ⓕ hide   Ⓗ hides

Ⓖ hiding   Ⓙ were hiding

7 **Jamal _____ for his brother to come home from work.**

Ⓐ was waiting   Ⓒ wait

Ⓑ waiting   Ⓓ to wait

Directions: For number 8, choose the best combined sentence.

8 **Have you ever been camping? Have you ever been fishing?**

Ⓕ Have you ever been camping and fishing?

Ⓖ Have you ever been camping and been fishing?

Ⓗ Have you ever been camping or have you ever been fishing?

Ⓙ Have you ever been camping or fishing?

Language Arts Practice

Directions: For numbers 9–11, choose the correct capitalization.

9 **Mr. rogers**

Ⓐ mr. Rogers

Ⓑ MR. rogers

Ⓒ Mr. rogers

Ⓓ Mr. Rogers

10 **rocky mountains**

Ⓕ Rocky mountains

Ⓖ Rocky Mountains

Ⓗ rocky Mountains

Ⓙ correct as is

11 **dr. and mrs. brown came to visit on Sunday afternoon.**

Ⓐ Dr. and mrs brown came to visit on Sunday afternoon.

Ⓑ Dr. and Mrs. Brown came to Visit on Sunday afternoon.

Ⓒ Dr. and Mrs. Brown came to visit on Sunday afternoon.

Ⓓ Dr. and Mrs. brown came to visit on Sunday afternoon.

Directions: Choose the correct spelling for numbers 12 and 13.

12 **samwich**

Ⓕ sanwich   Ⓗ sandwitch

Ⓖ sandwich   Ⓙ samwitch

13 **knifes**

Ⓐ kniffes   Ⓒ knifs

Ⓑ knifees   Ⓓ knives

Directions: Choose the correct answer for numbers 14 and 15.

14 **Which sentence is complete?**

Ⓕ jumped in the pool.

Ⓖ Jen and Pam.

Ⓗ Jen and Pam jumped in the pool.

Ⓙ in the pool.

15 **Which of the following is a fragment?**

Ⓐ April gave her dog a bath.

Ⓑ April gave Tito a bath.

Ⓒ Gave Tito a bath.

Ⓓ Tito got a bath.

Math: Draw a Diagram

Many standardized tests will ask you to solve math story problems. Sometimes these are also called word problems. Use the following strategies to help solve story problems quickly. Remember, though, not every strategy can be used with every story problem. You will have to choose the best strategy to use for each one.

Draw a Diagram

Sometimes it's helpful to draw a diagram to visualize the activity described in a story problem. Diagrams can help you understand a problem and figure out the correct answer.

EXAMPLE **Cassie, Tony, Jose, and Ling are standing in line for lunch. Ling is in front of Tony, Jose is behind Tony, and Cassie is behind Ling but before Tony. Who is last in line?**

Ⓐ Cassie Ⓑ Tony Ⓒ Jose Ⓓ Ling

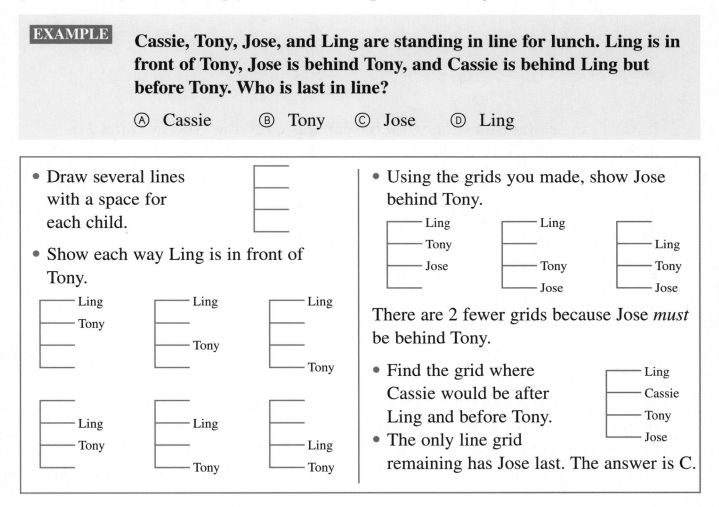

- Draw several lines with a space for each child.

- Show each way Ling is in front of Tony.

- Using the grids you made, show Jose behind Tony.

There are 2 fewer grids because Jose *must* be behind Tony.

- Find the grid where Cassie would be after Ling and before Tony.
- The only line grid remaining has Jose last. The answer is C.

When you draw a diagram:
- ☐ Read the problem carefully.
- ☐ Determine what data you need to solve the problem.
- ☐ Determine how to draw a diagram to organize the data.
- ☐ Draw a diagram based on the data in the problem.
- ☐ Solve the problem.

Diagram Practice

Directions: Draw a diagram in the space provided to help you solve each problem. Then choose the correct answer.

1 **Teri, Hank, Shawana, and Jimmy are the top finishers in a race. Teri finished before Hank, but after Shawana. Jimmy finished after Teri. Who won the race?**

Ⓐ Shawana   Ⓒ Teri

Ⓑ Hank   Ⓓ Jimmy

2 **In town, the restaurant is between the car wash and the grocery store. The grocery store is before the bank, but after the car wash. What is the order of the shops as you go down the street?**

Ⓕ restaurant, bank, car wash, grocery

Ⓖ bank, car wash, restaurant, grocery

Ⓗ car wash, restaurant, grocery, bank

Ⓙ car wash, bank, restaurant, grocery

3 **In our solar system Mercury is closest to the sun. Earth is between Venus and Mars. Venus is after Mercury, Jupiter is after Mars, but before Saturn. Uranus, Neptune, and Pluto are after Saturn. What is the fourth planet from the sun?**

Ⓐ Earth   Ⓒ Saturn

Ⓑ Mars   Ⓙ Uranus

Math: Trick Questions

Sometimes you're given trick questions on tests. These questions provide extra information that is not needed to solve the problem. You can deal with these questions by identifying the information required to solve the problem and setting aside the extra information that is unnecessary.

EXAMPLE **In the forest, 8 squirrels collected acorns from 9 trees. They collected 47 acorns from each tree. How many acorns did the squirrels collect in all?**

    Ⓐ   376 acorns   Ⓒ   423 acorns

    Ⓑ   705 acorns   Ⓓ   498 acorns

- To solve this problem, first determine what information you need to answer the question asked:
  How many acorns were collected?

- You need to know how many acorns from each tree the squirrels collected and the number of trees they collected them from. However, you do not need to know how many squirrels were collecting acorns to solve the problem.

$47 \times 9 = 423$ acorns

- You know the squirrels collected 423 acorns.
  The answer is **C**.

- The number of squirrels is extra information included in the problem to trick you. Be careful not to use this information to solve the problem.

When you think you have extra information:
- ☐ Read the problem carefully.
- ☐ Determine what information you need to solve the problem.
- ☐ Check for extra information.
- ☐ Set the extra information aside so you don't use it by mistake.
- ☐ Solve the problem.

Trick Questions Practice

Directions: Solve these problems. If there is extra information, write it in the space provided. Choose the correct answer.

1 Cody played in 3 basketball games last week. In the first game he scored 17 points, in the second game he scored 22 points, and in the third game he scored 19 points. How many points did he score last week?

Extra information:_____

_____

Ⓐ 48   Ⓒ 58

Ⓑ 61   Ⓓ 51

2 Jason bought 48 apples, 36 oranges, and 24 bananas for the fruit stand at the school fair. All of the apples were sold. If only 4 people bought apples, and each person bought the same number of apples, how many apples did each person buy?

Extra information:_____

_____

Ⓕ 12 apples

Ⓖ 9 apples

Ⓗ 27 apples

Ⓙ 6 apples

3 A recipe needs $\frac{1}{3}$ cup of white sugar, $\frac{2}{3}$ cup of brown sugar, 2 eggs, and $\frac{1}{3}$ cup of flour. How many cups of dry ingredients does the recipe use?

Extra information:_____

_____

Ⓐ $1\frac{1}{3}$ cups   Ⓒ $3\frac{1}{3}$ cups

Ⓑ $1\frac{2}{3}$ cups   Ⓓ 1 cup

4 Every day for a week Colleen practiced piano for 30 minutes. How long did she practice during the week?

Extra information:_____

_____

Ⓕ 2 hours, 30 minutes

Ⓖ 7 hours

Ⓗ 1 hour, 30 minutes

Ⓙ 3 hours, 30 minutes

Math: Paper and Pencil

It often helps to work through problems using paper and pencil. By working out a problem this way you can see and check the work you have done. Using paper and pencil is helpful when you have a *multi*-step problem on a test. You can do the first part of the problem and then carry that work on to the second part of the problem.

EXAMPLE **Mr. Simms has four boxes. In each of the boxes there are 16 candles. Mr. Simms wants to use all of his candles and put an equal number on each of 8 tables. How many candles will be on each table?**

Ⓐ 64 candles   Ⓒ 32 candles

Ⓑ 8 candles   Ⓓ 56 candles

- There are two parts to the problem. First, you have to multiply to find out how many candles there are altogether. Then, you have to divide to find out how many will be on each table.

- Use paper and pencil to multiply 16 ×4. This is the total number of candles.

$$\begin{array}{r} {\scriptstyle 2} \\ 16 \\ \times 4 \\ \hline 64 \text{ candles} \end{array}$$

- Then, use paper and pencil again to take the answer from the first part of the problem and solve the second part of the problem.

$$\begin{array}{r} 8 \quad \text{candles on each table} \\ 8\overline{)64} \\ -64 \\ \hline 0 \end{array}$$

- You now know that there are 8 candles on each table. The answer is **B**.

When you use pencil and paper:
- ☐ Read the problem carefully.
- ☐ Write neatly so that you do not make errors.
- ☐ Solve the problem.

Paper and Pencil Practice

Directions: Solve these problems using paper and pencil.
Do your work in the space provided.

1 There are 8 classrooms at Tanglewood Elementary School that have 17 students in them. There are 7 classrooms that have 18 students in them. How many students are there in all 15 classrooms?

Ⓐ 126 students   Ⓒ 136 students

Ⓑ 262 students   Ⓓ 321 students

2 At the county fair there are 2 dunking booths, 16 rides, 4 shows, 21 games, and 1 hall of mirrors. How many attractions are at the county fair altogether?

Ⓕ 44 attractions   Ⓗ 43 attractions

Ⓖ 23 attraction   Ⓙ 32 attractions

3 Taina had a rectangle made out of paper. She drew a line down the middle of the rectangle and then she drew a line diagonal through the rectangle. She then had 4 shapes drawn. What is one shape she made?

Ⓐ Square   Ⓒ Triangle

Ⓑ Circle   Ⓓ Oval

4 Julie bought a model robot building kit for $135 and a model rocket building kit for $128. She started with $350. How much money does she have left?

Ⓕ $215   Ⓗ $87

Ⓖ $222   Ⓙ $78

Math: Guess and Check

One way to solve word problems is to make a guess based on the information in the problem. Then you check it and revise your guess until you find the correct answer.

EXAMPLE **You have 7 coins that total $0.92. What combination of coins do you have?**

Ⓐ 2 quarters, 2 dimes, 1 nickel, 2 pennies

Ⓑ 3 quarters, 1 dime, 1 nickel, 2 pennies

Ⓒ 1 quarter, 3 dimes, 2 nickels, 1 penny

Ⓓ 2 quarters, 1 dime, 2 nickels, 3 pennies

• When you guess and check you need to try a set of numbers to see how close to $0.92 you can get.

Guess: 2 quarters, 2 dimes, 1 nickel, 2 pennies

$0.50 + 0.20 + 0.05 + 0.02 = $0.77

Check: $0.77 < $0.92

• Since your number was small, you should try larger numbers.

Guess: 3 quarters, 1 dime, 1 nickel, 2 pennies

$0.75 + 0.10 + 0.05 + 0.02 = $ 0.92

Check: $0.92 = 0.92

• Your guess is correct. The combination of 3 quarters, 1 dime, 1 nickel, and 2 pennies equals $0.92. The correct answer is **B**.

When you use guess and check:

☑ Read the problem carefully.

☑ Make a reasonable first guess.

☑ Revise your guess based on whether your answer was too high or low.

☑ Be sure your answer is reasonable based on the question.

Guess and Check Practice

Directions: Solve these problems using Guess and Check.

1 In Furry Friends Pet Store, one section of the store has parakeets and rabbits. There are 9 animals and 26 legs in that section of the store. How many 2 legged birds are there? How many 4 legged rabbits?

Ⓐ 5 parakeets, 4 rabbits

Ⓑ 4 parakeets, 3 rabbits

Ⓒ 2 parakeets, 5 rabbits

Ⓓ 6 parakeets, 1 rabbit

2 There are two numbers whose product is 81 and quotient is 9. What are the two numbers?

Ⓕ 9, 9

Ⓖ 3, 27

Ⓗ 7, 4

Ⓙ 4, 28

3 You have 4 coins that total $0.37. What combination of coins do you have?

Ⓐ 2 quarters, 2 pennies

Ⓑ 1 quarter, 1 dime, 2 pennies

Ⓒ 2 dimes, 1 nickel, 1 penny

Ⓓ 1 quarter, 1 dime, 2 pennies

4 Jane plants 2 packets of seeds in the garden. She plants a total of 26 seeds. Which 2 packets of seeds does she plant?

Ⓕ snapdragon and pansy

Ⓖ marigold and sunflower

Ⓗ sunflower and pansy

Ⓙ marigold and snapdragon

5 A shirt costs $10.99, pants cost $16.99, a sweater costs $14.99, and socks cost $4.99. What can Jim buy with $20.00?

Ⓐ sweater and shirt

Ⓑ pants and socks

Ⓒ sweater and socks

Ⓓ shirt and pants

Math: Estimation

On multiple choice tests you can estimate the answer as a way to cross off some of the choices. This makes it easier for you to find the correct answer.

EXAMPLE **Jackson spent $44.53 on summer clothes for camp. How much change will he receive after giving the sales clerk $50.00?**

Ⓐ $4.57   Ⓒ $4.53

Ⓑ $5.47   Ⓓ $5.43

- First, estimate the answer by rounding. You should round to the most precise place needed for the problem. In this case, round to the nearest dime.
    $44.53 rounds to $44.50
    $50.00 - $44.50 = 5.50

- You can cross off choices **A** and **C** since they have a 4 rather than a 5 in the dollars place.

- Find the exact answer by subtracting:

$$\begin{array}{r} \$50.00 \\ -\ 44.53 \\ \hline \$\ 5.47 \end{array}$$

- His change is $5.47. The correct answer is **B**.

When you estimate:
- ❑ Read the problem carefully.
- ❑ Round the numbers you need.
- ❑ Estimate the answer.
- ❑ Cross off any answers not close to your estimate.
- ❑ Find the exact answer.

Estimation Practice

Directions: Solve these problems using estimation.

1 Dominic and Lucy raced against each other. Dominic finished in 24.8 seconds. Lucy finished in 22.6 seconds. How much faster was Lucy?

Ⓐ 1.2 seconds

Ⓑ 2.2 seconds

Ⓒ 2.1 seconds

Ⓓ 3.2 seconds

2 4,093 + 589 =

Ⓕ 4,682

Ⓖ 4,873

Ⓗ 4,573

Ⓙ 4,684

3 567 – 344 =

Ⓐ 233

Ⓑ 323

Ⓒ 223

Ⓓ 342

4 There are 98 houses in Jan's neighborhood. She delivers the newspaper to all but 75 of them. how many papers does she deliver?

Ⓕ 33

Ⓖ 23

Ⓗ 172

Ⓙ 13

5 On Saturday 564 people visited the zoo. On Sunday 678 people visited the zoo and on Monday 433 people visited the zoo. How many people in all visited the zoo?

Ⓐ 1,575

Ⓑ 1,721

Ⓒ 1,665

Ⓓ 1,675

Math: Incomplete Information

One of the answer choices for some problems on tests may be "not enough information." In this case, you may not be given all of the information you need to solve the problem. If you determine that you cannot solve the problem with the information given, you fill in the "not enough information" choice.

EXAMPLE   **Rosa and Ruben went to see a movie with their parents. The movie started at 4:30. The tickets were $6.00. After the movie they went to dinner and arrived home at 8:00. How long was the movie?**

Ⓐ 3 hours 30 minutes   Ⓒ 2 hours 30 minutes

Ⓑ 3 hours   Ⓓ not enough information

• Read the problem to find out the question you need to answer.
  How long was the movie?

• Determine what information you have.
  When Robin and Riley went to the movie
  The cost of the tickets
  What time they arrived home after dinner

• You do not have enough information to answer the question since you do not know the start and end times of the movie.

• Reread the problem to verify that you do not have enough information to solve the problem.

• You do not have enough information. Your answer is **D**.

When you think you have incomplete information:
- ☐ Read the problem carefully.
- ☐ Determine what information you need to solve the problem.
- ☐ Check to see if you have all the information to solve the problem.
- ☐ Make sure the information you need to solve the problem is missing.

Incomplete Information Practice

Directions: Solve these problems.

1 Five children were having pizza for dinner. Michael had 2 slices, Colby had 1 slice, Stacey had 3 slices, and Jorge had 2 slices. How many slices did Mark have?

Ⓐ 1 slice   Ⓒ 2 slices

Ⓑ 3 slices   Ⓓ not enough information

2 Mr. Hoy planted 45 seeds in the fall. He planted 20 tomato seeds, 15 cucumber seeds, and the rest were for onions. How many seeds were for onions?

Ⓕ 15 seeds   Ⓗ 10 seeds

Ⓖ 12 seeds   Ⓙ not enough information

3 A hot air balloon stayed afloat for 25 minutes. The crew wanted to take a hot air balloon ride that last 40 minutes. How many tanks of gas would they need?

Ⓐ 1 tank   Ⓒ 3 tanks

Ⓑ 5 tanks   Ⓓ not enough information

4 Miss Cohen teaches piano lessons to 7 students every day. Each lesson lasts thirty minutes. How many minutes does Miss Cohen teach each day?

Ⓕ 3 hours   Ⓗ 7 hours

Ⓖ 3 hours 30 minutes   Ⓙ not enough information

5 There were 12 people in the public swimming pool. How many more people could be in the pool?

Ⓐ 57 people   Ⓒ 45 people

Ⓑ 33 people   Ⓓ not enough information

Math: Use a Calculator

You may be allowed to use a calculator with some standardized tests. Using a calculator can save you time, especially when you need to compute multi-digit numbers. A calculator also allows you to quickly check your work.

EXAMPLE   **The forest service in Red Park plants 322 new trees every year for 14 years. How many trees were planted in all over 14 years?**

Ⓐ 5,609   Ⓒ 4,508

Ⓑ 12,408   Ⓓ 4,216

• To solve the problem, you need to multiply a three-digit number by a two-digit number. It is quicker and easier to use your calculator, especially on a timed test.

$$322 \times 14$$

• They planted 4,508 trees. The answer is **C**.
• When you use a calculator you make a complex problem easier, but you must be sure to key in the correct numbers to find the correct answer.

When you use a calculator:
  ☑ Read the problem carefully.
  ☑ Be sure you key in the correct numbers.
  ☑ Solve the problem.

Calculator Practice

Directions: Solve these problems using a calculator.

1 Delcia earned $654.32 every week at her job. How much did Delcia earn in 12 weeks?

- Ⓐ $5,216.89
- Ⓒ $7,851.84
- Ⓑ $7,345.81
- Ⓓ $7,867.84

2 A FleetAir airplane holds 186 passengers. FleetAir flies 12 filled airplanes each day. How many people ride FleetAir each day?

- Ⓕ 2,232 people
- Ⓗ 186 people
- Ⓖ 1,450 people
- Ⓙ 1,203 people

3 At the first performance of a play there were 806 people in the audience. On the second night there were 943 people in the audience. On the third night there were 1,034 people in the audience. How many people attended the show in all?

- Ⓐ 2,867 people
- Ⓒ 1,977 people
- Ⓑ 2,783 people
- Ⓓ 1,840 people

4 The movie theater holds 225 guests. If every seat is sold in the theater, how much money will the theater take in?

- Ⓕ $1,012.50
- Ⓗ $10,125.00
- Ⓖ $9,990.00
- Ⓙ $1,120.50

5 John and Susanna want to hike the entire Long Trail in Vermont in 3 trips. On the first trip they hiked 87 miles. On the second trip they hiked 105 miles. How many miles do they have left to hike?

- Ⓐ 192 miles
- Ⓑ 18 miles
- Ⓒ 9,135 miles
- Ⓓ 73 miles

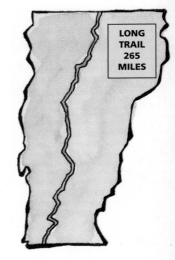

Math: Computation

Most standardized tests contain math sections where you must solve a variety of number equations. These questions test your ability to find exact answers to math problems. You will often be allowed to use scrap paper to work out these problems, but the work you show on scrap paper will not count.

The following is a list of skills that are often tested in the Computation segments of standardized tests. The list also contains tips for how to solve tough problems.

Using Operations

Your ability to perform basic mathematical operations (such as addition, subtraction, multiplication, and division) will be tested. Whenever you are solving a math equation, be sure of which operation you must use to solve the problem.

- Even though you will be given answer choices, it's best to work the problem out first using scrap paper. Then you can compare the answer you found to the choices that are given.
- If you have time, double-check your answer to each problem by using the inverse operation. If an equation requires you to add, for example, double-check your answer by substituting your answer choice for the appropriate part of the equation and then subtracting backwards.
- Keep in mind that the same equation may be written differently. Even though these problems look different, they ask you to do the exact same thing. Here are two equations for the same problem:

$$99 - 66 = ?$$

$$\begin{array}{r} 99 \\ -66 \\ \hline ? \end{array}$$

Other Things to Keep in Mind

- When using decimals, make sure your answer choice shows the decimal point in the correct place.
- If your problem contains units (such as 2 centimeters + 50 millimeters = X millimeters), be sure that you find the answer choice with the correct units labeled. Many tests will try to confuse you by substituting one unit for another in an answer choice.
- Finally, if you get to a tough problem, look carefully at the answer choices and use logic to decide which one makes the most sense. Then plug this choice into the equation and see if it works.

Computation Practice

Directions: Mark the letter of the answer to each problem below.

1   **5.91 − 2.39 =**

- Ⓐ   83
- Ⓑ   3.52
- Ⓒ   3.62
- Ⓓ   8.30

2   **647 + 692 =**

- Ⓕ   45
- Ⓖ   1239
- Ⓗ   1249
- Ⓙ   1339

3 $\frac{3}{4} + \frac{3}{4} =$

- Ⓐ   0
- Ⓑ $\frac{2}{4}$
- Ⓒ $1\frac{2}{4}$
- Ⓓ   6

4   **93 ×6 =**

- Ⓕ   99
- Ⓖ   109
- Ⓗ   548
- Ⓙ   558

5 $1\frac{1}{5} - \frac{4}{5} =$

- Ⓐ   2
- Ⓑ   1
- Ⓒ $\frac{2}{5}$
- Ⓓ $\frac{1}{5}$

6   **67 ×5 =**

- Ⓕ   350
- Ⓖ   335
- Ⓗ   62
- Ⓙ   13

7   **962 − 128 =**

- Ⓐ   834
- Ⓑ   844
- Ⓒ   846
- Ⓓ   1008

8   **$12.64 − $5.08 =**

- Ⓕ $6.56
- Ⓖ $7.66
- Ⓗ $7.56
- Ⓙ $7.76

Math: Concepts

Standardized tests also test your understanding of important math concepts you will have learned about in school. The following is a list of concepts that you may be tested on:

Number Concepts

• recognizing the standard and metric units of measure used for weighing and finding length and distance.
• recognizing place value (the ones, tens, hundreds, and thousands places; the tenths and hundredths places).
• telling time to the nearest quarter-hour.
• using a calendar.
• reading a thermometer.
• rounding up and down to the nearest ten or hundred.
• recognizing the bills and coins we use for money.

Geometry

• identify flat shapes such as triangles, circles, squares, rectangles, and more.
• identify solid shapes such as prisms, spheres, cubes, cylinders, and cones.
• find the perimeter of flat shapes.
• find the line of symmetry in a flat shape.
• tell about the number of angles and sides of flat shapes.

Other Things to Keep in Mind

• If you come to a difficult problem, think of what you do know about the topic and eliminate answer choices that don't make sense.
• Also keep in mind that you may be given a problem that can't be solved because not enough information is provided. In that case, "not enough information" or "none of the above" will be an answer choice. Carefully consider each of the other answer choices before you decide that a problem is not solvable.

Concept Practice

Directions: Find the answer to each problem below.

1 **What time does this clock show?**

Ⓐ 9:45

Ⓑ 10:15

Ⓒ 10:45

Ⓓ 11:00

2 **What place does the 7 hold in this number? 3070.5**

Ⓕ tenths place

Ⓖ ones place

Ⓗ tens place

Ⓙ hundreds place

3 **Round the number 46 up to the nearest ten:**

Ⓐ 40

Ⓑ 45

Ⓒ 50

Ⓓ 100

4 **Find the perimeter of a square with one side of $7\frac{1}{2}$ feet.**

Ⓕ 15

Ⓖ 28

Ⓗ 30

Ⓙ not enough information

5 **Which of these letters is not symmetrical?**

Ⓐ H

Ⓑ O

Ⓒ Z

Ⓓ X

6 **How many minutes are there in one day?**

Ⓕ 24

Ⓖ 60

Ⓗ 720

Ⓙ 1440

Math: Applications

You will often be asked to apply what you know about math to a new type of problem or set of information. Even if you aren't exactly sure how to solve a problem of this type, you can usually draw on what you already know to make the most logical choice.

When preparing for standardized tests, you may want to practice some of the following:

- how to use a number line.
- putting numbers in order from least to greatest and using greater than/less than symbols.
- recognizing basic number patterns and object patterns and extending them.
- choosing the best operation to solve a problem and writing an equation to solve the problem.
- reading bar graphs, tally charts, or pictographs.
- reading pie charts.
- reading simple line graphs.
- reading and making Venn diagrams.

Other Things to Keep in Mind

- When answering application questions, be sure to read each problem carefully. You may want to use scrap paper to work out some problems.
- Again, if you come to a problem you aren't sure how to solve or a word/idea you don't recognize, try to eliminate answer choices by using what you do know. Then go back and check your answer choice in the context of the problem.

Application Practice

Directions: Find the answer to each problem below.

1 What is the next number in this pattern? 2, 4, 8, 16, 32, _____

(A) 36   (C) 64

(B) 60   (D) 128

2 How many more students voted for chocolate ice cream than strawberry?

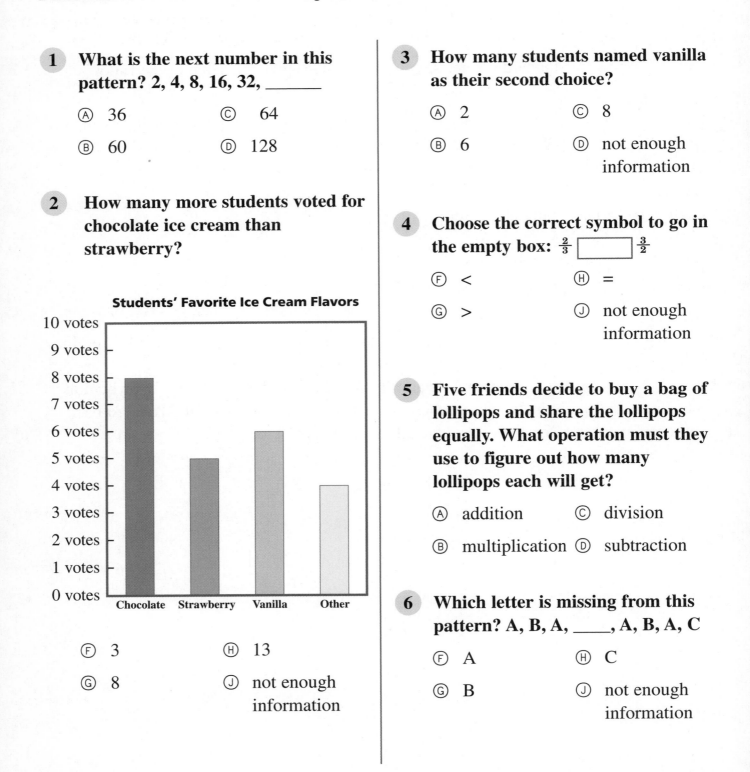

Students' Favorite Ice Cream Flavors

(F) 3   (H) 13

(G) 8   (J) not enough information

3 How many students named vanilla as their second choice?

(A) 2   (C) 8

(B) 6   (D) not enough information

4 Choose the correct symbol to go in the empty box: $\frac{2}{3}$ ☐ $\frac{3}{2}$

(F) <   (H) =

(G) >   (J) not enough information

5 Five friends decide to buy a bag of lollipops and share the lollipops equally. What operation must they use to figure out how many lollipops each will get?

(A) addition   (C) division

(B) multiplication   (D) subtraction

6 Which letter is missing from this pattern? A, B, A, _____, A, B, A, C

(F) A   (H) C

(G) B   (J) not enough information

Social Studies

Standardized tests often include questions about social studies topics. You may see questions about maps, geography, history, and government.

The following is a list of topics that may be covered on the test and tips to use when answering the questions. Sample questions are also included.

Map Skills

You will probably be asked to read a map and to identify some of its parts:

- **compass rose:** shows where north, south, east, and west are
- **legend**, or **map key:** shows **symbols** (drawings) that represent natural or human-made objects
- **scale:** compares distance on the map to actual distance

You may also be asked to think about other mapping tools, such as charts, atlases, and globes, as well as map vocabulary, such as **pole**, **equator**, **hemisphere**, and **continent**.

Geography

Geography is the study of the land and its features. Keep in mind some of the basic geography words:

- **natural features:** plateau, mountain, ocean, bay, peninsula, island
- **man-made features**: bridges, roads, buildings, aqueducts

Social Studies

Time Lines

A time line organizes historical events in the order in which they occurred. It is a helpful picture that can help you figure out which events happened first, and which happened later. Some questions will ask you to use a timeline to answer a question:

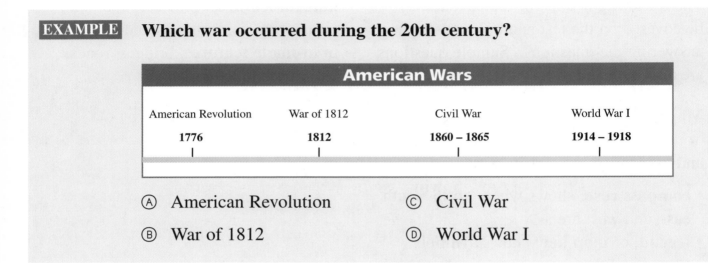

EXAMPLE **Which war occurred during the 20th century?**

American Wars			
American Revolution	War of 1812	Civil War	World War I
1776	1812	1860 – 1865	1914 – 1918

Ⓐ American Revolution   Ⓒ Civil War

Ⓑ War of 1812   Ⓓ World War I

The correct answer is **D** because the 20th century lasted from 1901-2000. World War I is the only war that took place during this time.

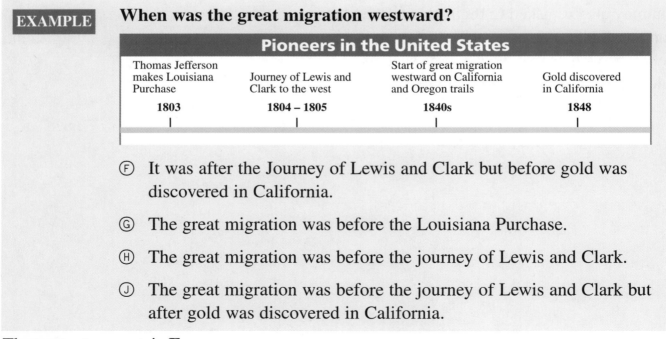

EXAMPLE **When was the great migration westward?**

Pioneers in the United States			
Thomas Jefferson makes Louisiana Purchase	Journey of Lewis and Clark to the west	Start of great migration westward on California and Oregon trails	Gold discovered in California
1803	1804 – 1805	1840s	1848

Ⓕ It was after the Journey of Lewis and Clark but before gold was discovered in California.

Ⓖ The great migration was before the Louisiana Purchase.

Ⓗ The great migration was before the journey of Lewis and Clark.

Ⓙ The great migration was before the journey of Lewis and Clark but after gold was discovered in California.

The correct answer is **F**.

Social Studies

Reading Passages

You will probably be asked to read a passage about a social studies topic and to answer questions about it. An excellent strategy is to read the questions before you read the passage, so that you know what to look for. Remember that some questions will ask you to look for specific facts, while other questions might ask you to use the information in the passage to draw your own conclusions.

Cause and Effect

Some questions will ask you to think about the causes or effects of historical events. Use your common sense as you answer these questions, and try to cross off the unreasonable answers before you make your choice.

EXAMPLE **Which of the following is a possible effect of a drought?**

Ⓐ heavy thunderstorms

Ⓑ lack of food

Ⓒ plentiful crops

Ⓓ many flowers

Since a drought is an extended period of time without rain, you can easily cross off **A**, **C**, and **D**, which all require rain. The correct answer is **B**, since a lack of rain would prevent crops from growing.

Social Studies Knowledge

Some social studies questions will ask specific questions about topics you have been studying in class, such as:

• Native Americans
• American government and its leaders
• early settlers in North America

As you answer these questions, be sure to make sure you understand what each question is asking. Get rid of the unreasonable answers first. Then make your best guess.

Social Studies Practice

Directions: For questions 1–3, study the map and answer the questions that follow.

1 What is the capital of Millenia?

Ⓐ Parkerville   Ⓒ Toluca

Ⓑ Carson   Ⓓ Wilbury

2 In which direction would you travel to get from Parkerville to Toluca?

Ⓕ north   Ⓗ east

Ⓖ south   Ⓙ west

3 Which town is located on a peninsula?

Ⓐ Parkerville   Ⓒ Toluca

Ⓑ Carson   Ⓓ Wilbury

Directions: For questions 4–6, find the correct answer.

4 The _____ is an imaginary horizontal line drawn around the center of the earth.

Ⓕ globe

Ⓖ equator

Ⓗ hemisphere

Ⓙ North Pole

5 A government in which the leaders are elected is called a

Ⓐ monarchy.

Ⓑ oligarchy.

Ⓒ democracy.

Ⓓ theocracy.

6 Which of the following was probably not a result of the invention of the telephone?

Ⓕ People wrote fewer letters.

Ⓖ News traveled faster.

Ⓗ People communicated more frequently.

Ⓙ People walked over to each other's houses more frequently.

Social Studies Practice

Directions: For numbers 7 and 8, read the passage and answer the questions that follow.

August 19, 1874

Dear Will,

By the time this letter reaches you, I will have reached California. It has taken us so many weeks, and I am eager for our journey to be over.

We are passing through Blackfoot territory these days. Last week, we saw one of their villages, with their cone-shaped homes made from buffalo skin in a circle around a central fire. At night, the firelight glows through the hides, and it is quite beautiful. Though their homes are so different from ours, it made me wish for a home of our own. I cannot wait to reach the West!

Your friend,

Silas

7 Silas is probably

   Ⓐ a Blackfoot Indian.

   Ⓑ a settler moving to the East Coast.

   Ⓒ a settler moving to the West Coast.

   Ⓓ living in the Midwest

8 A Blackfoot home is called a

   Ⓕ tipi.

   Ⓖ wigwam.

   Ⓗ wetu.

   Ⓙ pueblo.

Science

You will often see science questions on standardized tests. These questions may be about scientific facts. They may also test your ability to "think like a scientist." This means you must use data (information) to make predictions and draw conclusions.

The following list of tips includes some words you will need to know. It also contains examples of the types of science questions you may see on a test.

Science Words

Many science questions will include at least one of the words below:

- **research question**: the question that a scientist asks (*How does sunlight affect plants?*)
- **hypothesis:** a scientist's possible answer to the question (*If there is not enough sunlight, the plants will not grow.*)
- **experiment:** a test to see if the hypothesis is correct
- **prediction:** a guess about the future results of an experiment (*The plants with more sunlight will be taller than the plants with less sunlight.*)
- **observation:** when a scientist watches the results of an experiment
- **data:** the information collected in an experiment (*The plant grew 3 inches this month.*)
- **conclusion:** a statement based on information gathered in an experiment (*Sunlight helps plants to grow.*)

Science Knowledge

Science questions on your standardized test may require you to know specific information about various topics in science. These topics may include:

- the solar system.
- the life of a plant.
- the water cycle.
- endangered species.
- conservation.
- rocks and minerals.

If you don't know the answer to a specific question, use your common sense. The best strategy is to get rid of unreasonable answers before you make your choice.

Science

Reading Graphs

Standardized tests may include graphs showing the results of an experiment. You may be asked to read the data on the graph or to use the data to make a prediction or draw a conclusion.

EXAMPLE

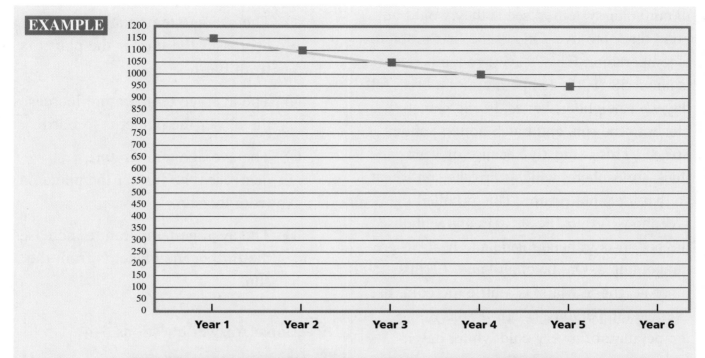

Based on the data in the graph above, what would be an accurate prediction for the panda population in year 6?

Ⓐ 1,000   Ⓒ 1050

Ⓑ 950   Ⓓ 900

Pandas decrease by 50 each year. The prediction for Year 6 would be 900, 50 less than 950 in Year 5. So the answer is **D**.

What is the difference in panda populations between year 1 and year 6?

Ⓕ 150   Ⓗ 1050

Ⓖ 250   Ⓙ 300

You know that the panda population for Year 6 is 900. In Year 1 it was 1150. 1150 – 900 is 250. So the answer is **G**.

Science Practice

Directions: For questions 1 and 2, read the passage and answer the questions that follow.

Scientists have looked at the other planets in our solar system to see if they would be good places to live. One of the first problems is temperature. Earth's average temperature is about 58 °F, the temperature of a brisk fall day. Our neighbor, Venus, is one planet closer to the sun, and much hotter—about 867 °F! This is mostly because of Venus's thick atmosphere, which traps the sun's heat so that it cannot escape. This is called the greenhouse effect, because in a greenhouse, the hot air is trapped inside and heats to great temperatures. On the other hand, Earth's other neighbor, Mars, is a little too cold. Its average temperature is ⁻13 °F, the temperature of a very cold winter day in Chicago!

1 Which of the following items would be a good example of the greenhouse effect?

Ⓐ a parked car on a summer day with the windows open

Ⓑ a parked car on a summer day with the windows closed

Ⓒ a parked car on a summer day with the air conditioning on

Ⓓ a running car on a summer day with the air conditioning on

2 From the information in the passage, which statement about planets' temperatures is probably true?

Ⓕ The average temperature decreases the further the planet is from Earth.

Ⓖ The average temperature increases the closer the planet is to Earth.

Ⓗ The average temperature decreases the further the planet is from the sun.

Ⓙ The average temperature increases the further the planet is from the sun.

Directions: Answer questions 3–4.

3 What tool would you use to examine a plant leaf in more detail?

Ⓐ a thermometer   Ⓒ a beaker

Ⓑ a scale   Ⓓ a microscope

4 Which of these is not a mammal?

Ⓕ lizard   Ⓗ dog

Ⓖ giraffe   Ⓙ whale

Practice Test and Final Test Information

The remainder of this book is made up of two tests. On page 75, you will find a Practice Test. On page 119, you will find a Final Test. These tests will give you a chance to put the tips you have learned to work.

Here are some things to remember as you take these tests:

- Be sure you understand all the directions before you begin each test.

- Ask an adult questions about the directions if you do not understand them.

- Work as quickly as you can during each test. There are no time limits on the Practice Test, but you should try to make good use of your time. There are suggested time limits on the Final Test to give you practice managing your time.

- You will notice little GO and STOP signs at the bottom of the test pages. When you see a GO sign, continue on to the next page if you feel ready. The STOP sign means you are at the end of a section. When you see a STOP sign, take a break.

- When you change an answer, be sure to erase your first mark completely.

- You can guess at an answer or skip difficult items and go back to them later.

- Use the tips you have learned whenever you can.

- After you have completed your tests, check your answers with the answer key. You can record the number of questions you got correct for each unit on the recording sheet on page 158.

- It is OK to be a little nervous. You may even do better.

- When you complete all the lessons in this book, you will be on your way to test success!

Table of Contents

Practice Test

Final Test

Lesson 1   Story Reading

Suzie and Luis were up before their parents. They went outside the tent and looked at the sun coming up over the mountains.

Find the picture that shows where Suzie and Luis were.

at the beach   in the mountains   in the desert
Ⓐ   Ⓑ   Ⓒ

SAMPLE
B

Find the words that best complete the sentence.

Orange juice _____ .

tastes good   from trees   for breakfast
Ⓕ   Ⓖ   Ⓗ

Look at each answer choice before marking the one you think is right.

Skip difficult items and come back to them later. Take your best guess when you don't know which answer is right.

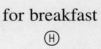

For many people, morning is the best time of the day. The stories and poem you will read next will talk about some of the things that make mornings special.

GO

Directions: This is a story about a family vacation. Read the story and then do numbers 1–7.

We're Not in Kansas Anymore

"I guess we're not in Kansas any more." Suzie smiled at her younger brother and walked toward the creek. Luis ran to catch up with her and took her hand. Both were wearing heavy sweaters to keep warm in the chilly morning air.

They sat down on a boulder beside the mountain stream. Across the stream was a meadow, and beyond that was a rocky base of a huge mountain. In fact, they were surrounded by mountains, many of which still had snow on them.

"Look, Suzie, cows." Luis pointed at several animals that had wandered into the meadow.

"I don't think they are cows, Buddy. They look like elk. I think they are almost like deer, but bigger."

Luis snuggled closer to his sister. He loved it when she called him "Buddy," and he was convinced she was the smartest person in the world, or at least the smartest kid.

GO

The family had arrived the night before at the campground. Mr. and Mrs. Montoya had set the tent up while the kids were sleeping in the back of the car. They woke the children up and helped them into their sleeping bags, but neither Suzie nor Luis had taken a look around. This morning was their first chance to see where they had camped.

As the sun rose higher over the top of the mountain, fish started dimpling the surface of the pool below the boulder on which the children sat. Each time the fish rose to the surface, they left a small ring of water that spread across the pond. As the rings bumped into one another, they made glittering patterns in the sunlight.

"I wonder what the fish are doing?" wondered Suzie out loud.

"Probably eating breakfast," answered a voice. They turned to see their mother standing behind them.

Mrs. Montoya hugged the children, and the three of them watched the fish quietly for a few minutes.

"Let's head back to the tent." suggested Mrs. Montoya. "Maybe we can convince Dad to cook us some breakfast. We have a busy day ahead of us."

1 The children in this story seem to

Ⓐ spend very little time together.

Ⓑ enjoy visiting their relatives.

Ⓒ love each other very much.

2 Luis calls the elk cows because

Ⓕ he doesn't know what elk are.

Ⓖ he is making a joke.

Ⓗ they look like deer.

GO

3 **Which of these will the children probably do next?**

Ⓐ walk over to the elk

Ⓑ eat breakfast

Ⓒ set up the tents

4 **Find the sentence that best completes the story.**

Mr. Montoya is fixing breakfast. _____ . Then he will cook pancakes.

Ⓕ He is getting his fishing rod ready.

Ⓖ The tent is large enough for the family.

Ⓗ First he will make a fire.

5 **Find the word that best completes the sentence.**

Mount Wheeler is the _____ peak in New Mexico.

Ⓐ high   Ⓑ higher   Ⓒ highest

6 **The children wore sweaters in the** chilly **morning air. A word that means the** *opposite* **of** chilly **is**

Ⓕ warm   Ⓖ cool   Ⓗ damp

7 **The meadow was at the base of a** rocky **cliff. Find another word that means** rocky.

Ⓐ dirty   Ⓑ stony   Ⓒ swampy

GO

Directions: This story is about a girl who spends each Saturday morning with her uncle. Read the story and then do numbers 8–12.

 Skim the story then skim the questions. Answer the easiest question first.

A Saturday Morning Surprise

Almost every Saturday morning, Uncle Bob stopped by Vanna's apartment to pick her up. Uncle Bob was her mother's older brother and had been her father's best friend. Vanna missed her father since he died a few years ago, but she was glad she had Uncle Bob.

On this Saturday morning, Uncle Bob said he had a surprise for Vanna. After saying good-bye to her mother, they took the elevator down to the street. Instead of getting in the car, she and Uncle Bob walked down the entrance to the subway and got on the next car that came by. They rode for about 15 minutes, then got off at a stop Vanna had never visited before. They walked up the stairs to the exit, and Vanna found herself in front of a building with huge columns holding up the roof.

"This is the Museum of Natural History, Vanna. It has some of the neatest things you could imagine. I thought you might enjoy spending the day here."

Vanna was speechless as they walked up the steps and through the doors. There, in the middle of a huge hallway, was a dinosaur skeleton! She and Uncle Bob walked over to a museum guide who was telling the story of the dinosaur. Vanna hung on every word she said, and when the guide had finished, Vanna was able to ask some questions.

Uncle Bob then led her over to another room. It was warm and dark, but at the far end there was a glow of light. As they got closer, a recording said, "Welcome to the Living Volcano." This room was just like being inside a real volcano. Vanna loved science, and she was sure this was going to be one of the best mornings ever with Uncle Bob.

GO

8 Look at the squares to the right. They show some of the things that might be found in a natural history museum. One of the squares is empty. Find the sentence that tells something else that might be found in a natural history museum.

Ⓕ lightning display

Ⓖ famous paintings

Ⓗ old cars

Ⓙ live animals

9 The story says that "Vanna was speechless." What does that probably mean?

Ⓐ She was disappointed at the surprise.

Ⓑ Uncle Bob didn't give her a chance to talk.

Ⓒ She was so excited she didn't know what to say.

Ⓓ The museum guide did all the talking.

GO

10 **Vanna did some research about museums. Find the best topic sentence for her paragraph.**

_____. *Art museums and science museums are the most well-known. Museums have also been built for trains, cars, and even toys.*

Ⓕ Some museums are free.

Ⓖ Students often take trips to museums.

Ⓗ Art museums have many paintings.

Ⓙ There are several kinds of museums.

11 **In the story, the roof of the museum is held up by <u>columns</u>. The <u>columns</u> probably look like**

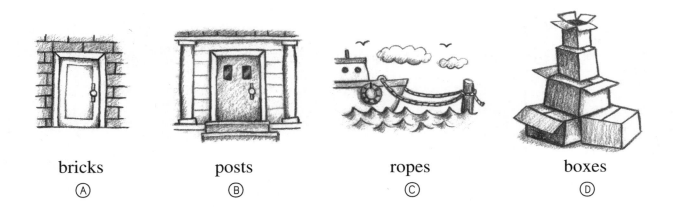

bricks   posts   ropes   boxes
Ⓐ   Ⓑ   Ⓒ   Ⓓ

12 **Find the sentence that is complete and correctly written.**

Ⓕ Crowded subway in the morning.

Ⓖ Museum opening at nine o'clock

Ⓗ They had breakfast before leaving.

Ⓙ Vanna getting ready early.

STOP

Lesson 2 Poem Reading

SAMPLE A

Every Monday, as we know,
Up we get, and off we go.

The writer is probably talking about going off to

Ⓐ school   Ⓑ dinner   Ⓒ shopping

Directions: Ben wrote this poem about something that couldn't happen. Read the poem and then do numbers 1–7.

What Do You Think?

I wonder if the sun gets tired
Of rising every day?
Or if the stars might want to see
How children like to play?

Perhaps the moon would like to learn
What children do in school?
Do they study very hard
And follow every rule?

Of course, these things can never be
Because it's nature's way,
For moon and stars to toil at night,
And sun to work all day.

The right answer is not always stated exactly in the poem.

1 **This poem is mostly about**

Ⓐ the moon and stars changing places with the sun.

Ⓑ children studying in school.

Ⓒ children pretending they are the sun, moon, or stars.

2 **This poem wonders if**

Ⓕ the moon is bored.

Ⓖ the stars are funny.

Ⓗ the sun is tired.

GO

3 In this poem, "nature's way" means

Ⓐ the way things are now.

Ⓑ the way things should be.

Ⓒ the way things were before.

4 Choose the words that best complete this sentence.

The moon _____.

Ⓕ shining at night

Ⓖ is bright tonight

Ⓗ in the dark sky

5 The moon and stars <u>toil</u> in the poem. Another word for <u>toil</u> is

Ⓐ play.

Ⓑ travel.

Ⓒ work.

6 Find the word that can take the place of <u>Millie and Larry</u> in the sentence below.

<u>Millie and Larry</u> went for a run this morning.

Ⓕ They

Ⓖ Them

Ⓗ It

7 Find the picture that shows what the moon is doing in the poem.

Ⓐ   Ⓑ   Ⓒ

GO

Directions: Ben started this poem. Help him finish it by choosing the right words to fill the blanks.

A cow is such a silly thing,
It makes a silly sound, _____ (8) _____
It lives on a _____ (9) _____
Inside a barn
And gives us milk, _____ (10) _____.

8 Ⓕ bark

　　Ⓖ meow

　　Ⓗ oink

　　Ⓙ moo

9 Ⓐ beach

　　Ⓑ farm

　　Ⓒ street

　　Ⓓ porch

10 Ⓕ too

　　Ⓖ also

　　Ⓗ yum

　　Ⓙ wow

Directions: For numbers 11 and 12, find the answer that best fills each blank.

A _____ (11) _____ is such a pretty thing,
with eyes and coat of brown.
It lives in the _____ (12) _____
And hides among trees
But rarely makes a sound.

11 Ⓐ (food name)

　　Ⓑ (person name)

　　Ⓒ (animal name)

　　Ⓓ (time name)

12 Ⓕ (place name)

　　Ⓖ (animal name)

　　Ⓗ (food name)

　　Ⓙ (time name)

13 **Which idea is <u>not</u> part of these poems?**

　　Ⓐ animal names

　　Ⓑ where animals live

　　Ⓒ animal sounds

　　Ⓓ what animals eat

STOP

Lesson 3 Writing

Directions: Read the paragraph about one student's favorite class. Then write one or two sentences to answer each question below.

> My favorite class is art. I like to draw, and I like to paint. The teacher is very nice. He shows us how to do new things. I always look forward to this class. It would be even better if it were longer.

What is your favorite class?

_____

_____

_____

_____

Why is it your favorite?

_____

_____

_____

_____

What might make this class even better?

_____

_____

_____

_____

GO

Directions: Read the short story about a friend's visit. Then think about a fiction story that you would like to write. Write one or two sentences to answer each question below.

Juan looked at the clock. He paced across the floor. His best friend, Bill, was coming to visit for the first time in six months. Bill had moved very far away. Juan wondered if they would still feel like good friends.

The doorbell rang, and Juan raced to answer it. Bill looked a bit unsure. Juan smiled and started talking just as he always had when they had lived near one another. He made Bill feel comfortable. As the day went on, it felt like old times.

Think about the main character. Who is it? What is he or she like?

_____

_____

_____

Where does the story take place? When does the story take place? Now? In the past? In the future?

_____

_____

_____

What problem will the main character have? How will he or she try to solve the problem?

_____

_____

_____

STOP

Lesson 4 **Review**

SAMPLE
A

The alarm clock at seven o'clock rang.

Which of these shows the best way to write this sentence?

Ⓐ At seven o'clock rang the alarm clock.

Ⓑ Rang at seven o'clock the alarm clock.

Ⓒ The alarm clock rang at seven o'clock.

Ⓓ Best as it is.

Directions: Nick wrote this story about birds coming to the feeder in his back yard in the morning. The story has a few errors that should be corrected. Read the story and then do numbers 1–4.

A Busy Morning

[1]The finches come to the feeder early. [2]They chirp and take turns eating. [3]Later, the doves them join. [4]The doves almost never eat at the feeder. [5]Instead, they pecking at seeds on the ground. [6]Another bird that eats on the ground is the junco. [7]Juncoes, they usually arrive in flocks of about ten. [8]They are shy birds and fly away if they see me.

GO

1 **Choose the best way to write Sentence 1.**

Ⓐ The finches comes to the feeder early.

Ⓑ Coming early to the feeder are the finches.

Ⓒ The finches had come to the feeder early.

Ⓓ Best as it is

2 **Which of these shows the best way to write Sentence 3?**

Ⓕ Later, the doves join they.

Ⓖ The doves join them later.

Ⓗ The doves join they later.

Ⓙ Best as it is

3 **Select the best way to write Sentence 5.**

Ⓐ Instead, they peck at seeds on the ground.

Ⓑ Them are pecking at seeds on the ground instead.

Ⓒ It pecks at seeds on the ground instead.

Ⓓ Best as it is

4 **Which of these shows the best way to write Sentence 7?**

Ⓕ Them juncoes usually arrive in flocks of about ten.

Ⓖ Juncoes are arriving usually in flocks of about ten.

Ⓗ Juncoes usually arrive in flocks of about ten.

Ⓙ Best as it is

GO

Directions: For numbers 5 and 6, find the sentence in each of these stories that has the correct capitalization and punctuation.

5 Ⓐ The bus comes for us at 7:30

Ⓑ terri likes to ride up front.

Ⓒ My friends and I sit in the back.

Ⓓ We talk about sports and television?

6 Ⓕ On saturday morning we sleep late.

Ⓖ Mom and Dad have to wake us.

Ⓗ the four of us have a big breakfast

Ⓙ Last week we went to denver.

7 One of Nick's friends wrote this story about the morning at his house. Find the best topic sentence for the story.

_____. *Both my mom and dad work, so they get in the bathroom first. My sister and I get up next. While we get ready, Dad fixes us breakfast.*

Ⓐ Morning in our house is very busy.

Ⓑ Breakfast is my favorite meal.

Ⓒ My sister and I like to sleep in.

Ⓓ We take a bus to school in the morning.

GO

8 **Nick's sister, Alex, wrote this story. Find the sentences that best complete it.**

Sometimes we go out for breakfast. Mom and Dad take us to different restaurants. _____.

Ⓕ They work downtown. Mom drives, but Dad takes the subway.

Ⓖ Breakfast is an important meal. You shouldn't eat too much.

Ⓗ I always order pancakes. Nick gets waffles.

Ⓙ Fruit is good to eat. I like bananas best.

Directions: For numbers 9 and 10, find the sentence that is complete and that is written correctly.

9 Ⓐ Mr. Woo his store early.

Ⓑ Always nice to us.

Ⓒ Food and other things.

Ⓓ We like to shop there.

10 Ⓕ Many people in the park.

Ⓖ Cool and smells good.

Ⓗ They run in the morning.

Ⓙ Later to get crowded.

11 **Find the words that best complete the sentence.**

_____ *all night long.*

Ⓐ It rained

Ⓑ Too hot to sleep

Ⓒ Cloudy and windy

Ⓓ A few times

STOP

Directions: Read the paragraph that describes a trip to the beach. Then think about a place you have visited. Write one or two sentences to answer each question below.

> I'll never forget my trip to the beach last summer. We drove a long time to get there. The sun blazed overhead. The sand felt hot against my feet. I splashed in the crashing waves and ate sweet, cool ice cream. I can't wait to go back to the beach!

What is the name of the place you visited?

_____

_____

_____

Did you like this place? Why or why not?

_____

_____

_____

_____

What do you remember about its sights, sounds, tastes, and smells?

_____

_____

_____

_____

_____

STOP

Basic Skills

Lesson 1 Word Analysis

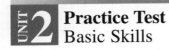

SAMPLE A

Find the word in which the underlined letters have the same sound as the picture name.

b̲read

Ⓐ

b̲lack

Ⓑ

b̲owl

Ⓒ

 Repeat the directions to yourself as you look at the answer choices. Think carefully about what you should do.

Directions: For numbers 1–4, choose the best answer.

1 Find the word that has the same beginning sound as

Ⓐ f̲rame.

Ⓑ f̲lame.

Ⓒ fork.

2 Find the word that has the same ending sound as

Ⓕ mean̲t.

Ⓖ stan̲d.

Ⓗ earn̲.

3 Look at the first word. Find the other word that has the same vowel sound as the underlined part.

f̲loat

Ⓐ block

Ⓑ board

Ⓒ chose

Ⓓ pool

4 Look at the underlined word. Find a word that can be added to the underlined word to make a compound word.

d̲oor

Ⓕ knock Ⓗ window

Ⓖ open Ⓙ step

STOP

Lesson 2 Vocabulary

Directions: For Samples A and B and numbers 1 and 2, find the answer that means the same or about the same as the underlined word.

SAMPLE A <u>consider</u> this idea

Ⓐ ignore   Ⓒ agree with

Ⓑ think about   Ⓓ like

SAMPLE B <u>raise</u> a flag

Ⓕ lift   Ⓖ lower

Ⓗ fly   Ⓙ hold

---

1 <u>liberty</u> for everyone

Ⓐ freedom   Ⓒ work

Ⓑ vacation   Ⓓ food

2 long <u>journey</u>

Ⓕ story   Ⓗ road

Ⓖ movie   Ⓙ trip

Directions: For number 3, find the word that means the opposite of the underlined word.

3 <u>thrilling</u> ride

Ⓐ long

Ⓑ exciting

Ⓒ boring

Ⓓ interesting

TIPS

Think about where you heard or read the underlined word before. Try each answer in the blank.

Directions: For numbers 4 and 5, read the sentence with the missing word and then read the question. Find the best answer to the question.

4 The weather will _____ tomorrow.

Which word means the weather will get better?

Ⓕ improve   Ⓗ worsen

Ⓖ change   Ⓙ vary

5 The _____ followed the rabbit into the forest.

Which word means a dog followed the rabbit into the forest?

Ⓐ traveler   Ⓒ hound

Ⓑ hunter   Ⓓ hawk

GO

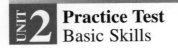
Directions: For Sample C and numbers 6 and 7, read the sentences. Then choose the word that correctly completes both sentences.

SAMPLE
C

The _____ swam in the pond.

You have to _____ your head here.

Ⓐ fish   Ⓑ duck   Ⓒ children   Ⓓ lower

6 Who will _____ this problem?

The _____ on the shovel is broken.

Ⓐ solve   Ⓑ blade   Ⓒ cause   Ⓓ handle

7 Can I take your _____?

She will _____ him to do it.

Ⓕ order   Ⓖ tell   Ⓗ coat   Ⓙ hat

 Use the meaning of the sentence to find the answer.

Directions: For numbers 8 and 9, read the story. For each blank, look at the words with the same number. Find the word from each list that fits best in the blank.

Dogs need __(8)__ to stay healthy. They should be given
an __(9)__ to play for at least 15 minutes each day.

8 Ⓐ exercise   Ⓑ leashes   Ⓒ treats   Ⓓ dishes

9 Ⓕ examination   Ⓖ assistance   Ⓗ individual   Ⓙ opportunity

STOP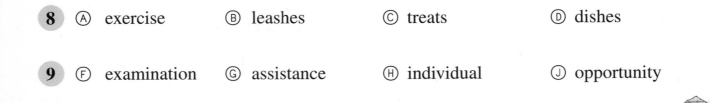

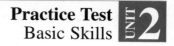
Lesson 3 — Language Mechanics

Directions: For Sample A and numbers 1 and 2, find the punctuation mark that is needed in the sentence.

SAMPLE A The television is too loud

- ? (A)
- . (B)
- , (C)
- None (D)

1 How many fish did you catch

- ? (A)
- . (B)
- , (C)
- None (D)

2 Quick, let's get out of the rain

- ? (F)
- . (G)
- ! (H)
- None (J)

Look for a mistake in capitalization or a missing punctuation mark in this part of the lesson.

Directions: For Sample B and numbers 3 and 4, which part needs a capital letter? If no capital letter is needed, mark "None."

SAMPLE B My cousin (A) | has a bird (B) | named fluffy. (C) | None (D)

3 Give this (A) | piece of pie (B) | to connie. (C) | None (D)

4 Imo's class (F) | will go to (G) | Orlando, Florida. (H) | None (J)

GO

Directions: Find the sentence that has the correct capitalization and punctuation.

5
   Ⓐ Our picnic is tomorrow!

   Ⓑ Mr. ames will cook.

   Ⓒ we'll meet Jenny there.

   Ⓓ Sam and I will be there.

6
   Ⓕ Who is playing.

   Ⓖ The park is this way!

   Ⓗ Call Jeff. He wants to come with us.

   Ⓙ The game starts soon. let's hurry

Remember, in this part of the lesson you should find the answer with correct capitalization and punctuation.

SAMPLE **C**

Find the answer choice that shows the correct capitalization and punctuation for the underlined part.

Did you finish your project. Mine is almost done.

   Ⓐ Project mine.

   Ⓑ project? Mine

   Ⓒ Project. Mine

   Ⓓ Correct as it is

Directions: For numbers 7 and 8, look at the underlined part of the sentence. Choose the answer that shows the best capitalization and punctuation for that part.

(7)   None of <u>Winnies friends</u> told her about the surprise
(8) birthday party. She was the captain of the softball <u>team. The</u> other players wanted to do something special for her.

7
   Ⓐ Winnies friend's

   Ⓑ Winnies' friends

   Ⓒ Winnie's friends

   Ⓓ Correct as it is

8
   Ⓕ team! The

   Ⓖ team the

   Ⓗ team, the

   Ⓙ Correct as it is

STOP

Lesson 4 Spelling

Directions: Find the word that is spelled correctly and best fits in the blank.

1 We picked _____ in our garden.

Ⓐ berries   Ⓒ berrys

Ⓑ berrese   Ⓓ berreis

2 The _____ helped me.

Ⓕ nourse   Ⓗ nurce

Ⓖ nirse   Ⓙ nurse

3 The answer to this problem is a _____ .

Ⓐ frackshun   Ⓒ fracteon

Ⓑ fraction   Ⓓ fracton

4 Did you _____ the page?

Ⓕ tare   Ⓗ tair

Ⓖ tear   Ⓙ taer

5 This _____ was in the school paper.

Ⓐ artical   Ⓒ article

Ⓑ articel   Ⓓ articol

Directions: For Sample A and numbers 6–8, find the underlined word that is <u>not</u> spelled correctly.

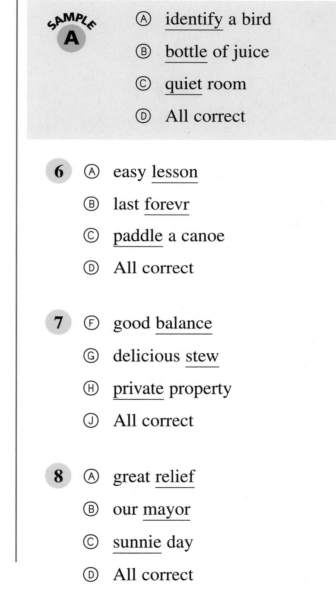

SAMPLE A

Ⓐ <u>identify</u> a bird

Ⓑ <u>bottle</u> of juice

Ⓒ <u>quiet</u> room

Ⓓ All correct

6 Ⓐ easy <u>lesson</u>

Ⓑ last <u>forevr</u>

Ⓒ <u>paddle</u> a canoe

Ⓓ All correct

7 Ⓕ good <u>balance</u>

Ⓖ delicious <u>stew</u>

Ⓗ <u>private</u> property

Ⓙ All correct

8 Ⓐ great <u>relief</u>

Ⓑ our <u>mayor</u>

Ⓒ <u>sunnie</u> day

Ⓓ All correct

If an item is too difficult, skip it and come back to it later.

STOP

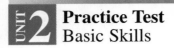

Lesson 5   Computation

Directions: For Samples A and B and numbers 1–4, find the answer that is the solution to the problem. If the answer is not given, choose "None of these."

SAMPLE **A**

23
+ 16

Ⓐ 17

Ⓑ 29

Ⓒ 39

Ⓓ 84

Ⓔ None of these

SAMPLE **B**

48
– 43

Ⓕ 10

Ⓖ 25

Ⓗ 41

Ⓙ 91

Ⓚ None of these

Pay attention to the operation sign so you know what to do.
Be sure to transfer numbers correctly to scratch paper.

1

$115 + 71 =$

Ⓐ 44

Ⓑ 76

Ⓒ 176

Ⓓ 186

Ⓔ None of these

3

$9.38
– 4.51

Ⓐ $4.87

Ⓑ $5.87

Ⓒ $5.32

Ⓓ $13.89

Ⓔ None of these

2

52
16
+ 5

Ⓕ 21

Ⓖ 57

Ⓗ 63

Ⓙ 83

Ⓚ None of these

4

$5 \times 5 =$

Ⓕ 10

Ⓖ 25

Ⓗ 35

Ⓙ 55

Ⓚ None of these

STOP

Lesson 6 Review

SAMPLE A Find the word in which the underlined letters have the same sound as the picture name.

Ⓐ s<u>k</u>ate Ⓑ s<u>m</u>ile Ⓒ s<u>l</u>ow

1 Find the word in which the underlined letters have the same sound as the picture name.

Ⓐ <u>st</u>amp

Ⓑ <u>sk</u>irt

Ⓒ <u>sw</u>an

2 Find the word that has the same ending sound as

Ⓕ ei<u>ght</u>.

Ⓖ len<u>gth</u>.

Ⓗ ra<u>nge</u>.

3 Look at the word. Find the other word that has the same vowel sound as the underlined part.

cr<u>i</u>sp

Ⓐ cried Ⓒ lion

Ⓑ stair Ⓓ pinch

4 Look at the underlined word. Find a word that can be added to the underlined word to make a compound word.   <u>hair</u>

Ⓕ dark Ⓗ comb

Ⓖ cut Ⓙ hat

5 Find the word in which just the prefix is underlined.

Ⓐ <u>pre</u>tend Ⓒ <u>be</u>tween

Ⓑ <u>al</u>low Ⓓ <u>un</u>known

6 Find the word in which only the root word is underlined.

Ⓕ <u>car</u>pet Ⓗ <u>bar</u>rel

Ⓖ <u>play</u>ful Ⓙ <u>re</u>lease

7 Find the word in which only the suffix is underlined.

Ⓐ land<u>ed</u> Ⓒ storm<u>s</u>

Ⓑ clos<u>et</u> Ⓓ tele<u>vision</u>

GO

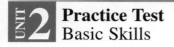
Directions: For Sample B and numbers 8 and 9, find the answer that means the same or about the same as the underlined word.

SAMPLE B

<u>firm</u> grip

- Ⓐ weak
- Ⓒ damp
- Ⓑ slippery
- Ⓓ strong

8 a good <u>pitch</u>

- Ⓐ catch
- Ⓒ hit
- Ⓑ throw
- Ⓓ score

9 <u>brush</u> a horse

- Ⓕ ride
- Ⓗ catch
- Ⓖ groom
- Ⓙ follow

SAMPLE C Find the answer that best fits in the blank.

Hector _____ his shirt on a thorn.

- Ⓐ tore
- Ⓒ handed
- Ⓑ folded
- Ⓓ grabbed

10 Which word means cutting the onions made Casper cry?

Cutting the onions made Casper _____.

- Ⓐ satisfied
- Ⓒ weep
- Ⓑ tired
- Ⓓ blush

Directions: Find the word that correctly completes both sentences.

11 Janna will _____ the table. This _____ of books is rare.

- Ⓕ clear
- Ⓗ move
- Ⓖ group
- Ⓙ set

12 My _____ is broken. Let's _____ a movie.

- Ⓐ watch
- Ⓒ rent
- Ⓑ toy
- Ⓓ radio

Directions: For each blank, look at the words with the same number. Find the word from each list that fits best in the blank.

Jim __(13)__ Michele's bike. His bike had a flat tire. He wouldn't be able to __(14)__ a new tire until next week.

13
- Ⓕ found
- Ⓗ borrowed
- Ⓖ lost
- Ⓙ disliked

14
- Ⓐ inflate
- Ⓒ purchase
- Ⓑ require
- Ⓓ express

GO

Directions: For Sample D and number 15, find the part of the sentence that needs a capital letter. Mark "None" if a capital letter is not needed.

SAMPLE D	This street	usually has	heavy traffic.	None
	Ⓐ	Ⓑ	Ⓒ	Ⓓ

15	Did carla	give you	her phone number?	None
	Ⓐ	Ⓑ	Ⓒ	Ⓓ

16 **Find the punctuation mark that is needed in the sentence.**

The mall is just up the road

?	.	,	None
Ⓕ	Ⓖ	Ⓗ	Ⓙ

Directions: For numbers 17 and 18, find the sentence that has correct capitalization and punctuation.

17
Ⓐ She and i will study now.

Ⓑ the library is closed.

Ⓒ Let's leave now?

Ⓓ Can Peg borrow your book?

18
Ⓕ Our coats' are wet.

Ⓖ Watch out for that ice!

Ⓗ What did you say.
I didn't hear you.

Ⓙ This desk is yours?
Mine is over there.

Directions: Read the letter. Find the answer that shows the correct capitalization and punctuation for the underlined parts.

(19) March 2 1998,
Dear Lena,
(20) Thanks for the football. I can't believe you sent it. I got other birthday presents, but yours was the best. I'll try it out tomorrow.
Your friend,
Ronnie

19
Ⓐ March, 2, 1998

Ⓑ March 2 1998

Ⓒ March 2, 1998

Ⓓ Correct as it is

20
Ⓕ cant   Ⓗ ca'nt

Ⓖ cant'   Ⓙ Correct as it is

GO

Directions: For Sample E and numbers 21 and 22, find the word that is spelled correctly and best fits in the blank.

> **SAMPLE E** My sister got _____ on that hill.
>
> Ⓐ maried   Ⓒ marreed
>
> Ⓑ married   Ⓓ marread

21 Jamie's _____ will be next week.

Ⓐ berthday   Ⓒ birthday

Ⓑ burthday   Ⓓ birthdey

22 At _____, we began our hike.

Ⓕ daun   Ⓗ dawn

Ⓖ dawne   Ⓙ dawen

Directions: Find the underlined word that is not spelled correctly. If all the words are correct, mark "All correct."

23 Ⓐ clear day   Ⓒ famous artist

Ⓑ gold medal   Ⓓ All correct

24 Ⓕ usefull hint   Ⓗ lock the door

Ⓖ go swimming   Ⓙ All correct

Directions: For Sample F and numbers 25–27 find the answer that is the solution to the problem. If the answer is not given, choose "None of these."

> **SAMPLE F**
>
> 40
> + 30
>
> Ⓐ 10
>
> Ⓑ 60
>
> Ⓒ 80
>
> Ⓓ None of these

25

$1.30 + 3.39

Ⓐ $2.09

Ⓑ $4.39

Ⓒ $4.69

Ⓓ None of these

26

$1.72
− .22

Ⓕ $1.40

Ⓖ $1.50

Ⓗ $1.94

Ⓙ None of these

27

700
×3

Ⓐ 1000

Ⓑ 2100

Ⓒ 7300

Ⓓ None of these

STOP

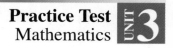
Lesson 1   Mathematics Skills

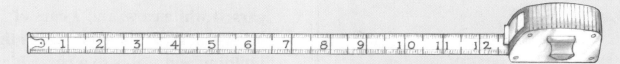

SAMPLE A

How many inches long is the fish?

Ⓐ 5 inches

Ⓑ 6 inches

Ⓒ 8 inches

Ⓓ 12 inches

TIPS

Read the problem carefully. Look for key words, numbers, and figures. Look carefully at all the answer choices.

If you use scratch paper, transfer the numbers correctly. Work neatly and carefully so you don't make a careless mistake.

GO

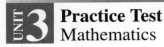
1 **What is the best estimate of the number of beans on the plate?**

Ⓐ 30

Ⓑ 20

Ⓒ 12

Ⓓ 10

2 **Look at the number pattern in the box. Find the number that is missing.**

11, 22, _____, 44, 55

Ⓕ 33

Ⓖ 23

Ⓗ 32

Ⓙ 42

3 **Look at the clock. How long will it take the minute hand to reach the 6?**

Ⓐ 3 minutes

Ⓑ 5 minutes

Ⓒ 12 minutes

Ⓓ 15 minutes

4 **Marlow noticed that the parking lot at the store had 11 red cars, 6 blue cars, 4 white cars, and 3 cars of other colors. If someone leaves the building and walks to a car, which color car is it most likely to be?**

Ⓕ red

Ⓖ blue

Ⓗ white

Ⓙ another color

5 **Sandy had 5** **.**

She read 2 **.**

Find the number sentence that tells how many books Sandy has left to read.

Ⓐ 5 + 2 = 7

Ⓑ 5 − 2 = 3

Ⓒ 2 + 3 = 5

Ⓓ 2 − 1 = 1

GO

6 Look at the pattern of fruit. Which of these is the missing piece of fruit?

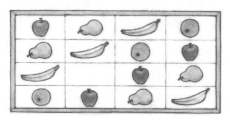

Ⓕ orange   Ⓗ pear

Ⓖ banana   Ⓙ apple

7 Mr. Lowell paid $0.59 for a bag of chips and $0.39 for a bottle of juice. How much money did he spend all together?

Ⓐ $0.79

Ⓑ $0.88

Ⓒ $0.89

Ⓓ $0.98

8 Look at the number sentences. Find the number that goes in the boxes to make both number sentences true.

$6 + \square = 7$
$7 - \square = 6$

Ⓕ 1

Ⓖ 0

Ⓗ 13

Ⓙ 7

9 Look at the picture. What number tells how many blocks are in the picture?

Ⓐ 100

Ⓑ 115

Ⓒ 110

Ⓓ 15

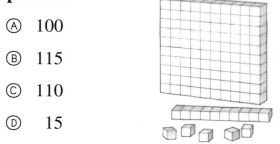

Directions: For numbers 10 and 11, estimate the answer to each problem. You do not have to find an exact answer.

10 Which two things together would cost about $30.00?

Ⓕ hat and shirt

Ⓖ belt and socks

Ⓗ shirt and socks

Ⓙ hat and belt

$18.00

$9.00

$13.00

11 Use estimation to find which of these is closest to 1000.

Ⓐ 591 + 573   Ⓒ 392 + 589

Ⓑ 499 + 409   Ⓓ 913 + 183

GO

Directions: The third grade students at Millbrook School made a graph about where they wanted to go on vacation. Study the graph, then do numbers 12–14.

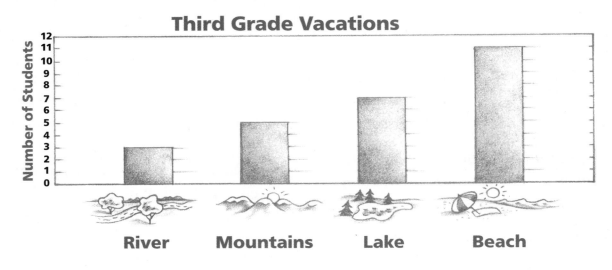

12 Which of these is another way to show how many students went to the beach?

- Ⓕ ⲧⲏⲧ ⲧⲏⲧ |
- Ⓖ ⲧⲏⲧ |
- Ⓗ ⲧⲏⲧ ⲧⲏⲧ
- Ⓙ ⲧⲏⲧ ⲧⲏⲧ ||/|

13 How many students went to a lake for vacation?

- Ⓐ 11
- Ⓒ 8
- Ⓑ 7
- Ⓓ 5

14 Two of the students changed their minds and decided to go to a lake instead of the beach. How many students then wanted to go to a lake?

- Ⓕ 7
- Ⓗ 5
- Ⓖ 8
- Ⓙ 9

GO

15 Look at the paper clip and the pencils. Which pencil is about three inches longer than the paper clip?

Ⓐ   Ⓑ   Ⓒ   Ⓓ

16 Bonnie folded a piece of paper in half and then folded it in half again. The picture shows how she folded her paper. What will the piece of paper look like when Bonnie unfolds it?

Ⓕ   Ⓖ   Ⓗ   Ⓙ

17 Find the answer that shows 35 peanuts.

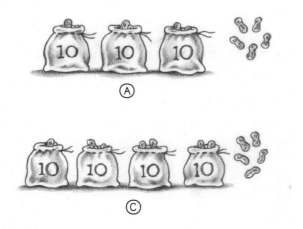

Ⓐ   Ⓑ

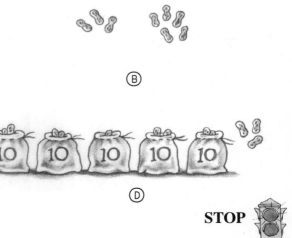

Ⓒ   Ⓓ

STOP

Lesson 2 Review

MAIN STREET FAIR

SAMPLE A Last week, two hundred fifty-three people attended the Main Street Fair. Which of these numbers is two hundred fifty-three?

Ⓐ 235   Ⓑ 20053   Ⓒ 253   Ⓓ 2053

Directions: Study the schedule for the Main Street Fair. Use it to do numbers 1 and 2.

Main Street Fair

8:00 – 10:00
Student-Teacher Softball Game
10:15 – 12:00
Arts and Crafts Sale
12:30 – 2:00
Cookout in the Park
2:30 – 4:00
Pet Show

1 Mrs. Barnes arrived 15 minutes early for the softball game. What time did she get there?

Ⓐ 8:15   Ⓒ 7:15

Ⓑ 8:45   Ⓓ 7:45

2 Exactly 60 people brought their pets to the show. Half the people brought dogs and 20 people brought cats. How many people brought other kinds of pets?

Ⓕ 30   Ⓗ 20

Ⓖ 10   Ⓙ 40

GO

3 Pepper's little brother made this castle with toy blocks. Which shape did he use just once?

Ⓐ circle

Ⓑ triangle

Ⓒ rectangle

Ⓓ square

4 The chart below shows the number of cars parked in a lot. Which of these is the same number as is shown on the chart?

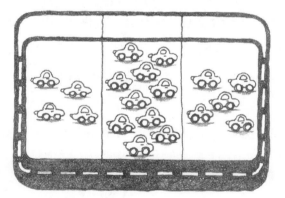

Ⓕ 100 + 40 + 5

Ⓖ 1 + 4 + 5

Ⓗ 400 + 100 + 5

Ⓙ 4 + 10 + 5

5 Paul and Vesta used a computer to solve a problem. Which of these is the same as the number on the computer screen?

Ⓐ three thousand one hundred eight

Ⓑ thirty one thousand eight

Ⓒ three hundred eight

Ⓓ three thousand eighteen

6 Sarah just read that her town has the highest population in the county. Where should she mark on the chart below to show her town's population?

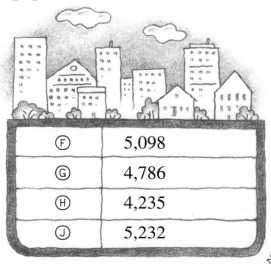

Ⓕ	5,098
Ⓖ	4,786
Ⓗ	4,235
Ⓙ	5,232

GO

Going to the Bank

The Dime Bank
Opens: 9:00
Closed: 4:00

7 **What do the numbers on the sign tell you?**

Ⓐ how much money is in the bank

Ⓑ how many people work in the bank

Ⓒ what time the bank opens and closes

Ⓓ the bank's address

8 **Jawan's sister has four coins. One is a nickel and one is a dime. Which of these amounts might she have?**

Ⓕ 15 cents   Ⓖ 20 cents   Ⓗ 24 cents   Ⓙ 30 cents

9 **A sticker costs 20 cents. Jawan has 12 cents. How much more money does he need to buy the sticker?**

Ⓐ 8¢

Ⓑ 10¢

Ⓒ 12¢

Ⓓ 32¢

20¢

STOP

Social Studies

Lesson 1

Directions: Study the time line that shows when four U. S. Presidents took office.
Then do numbers 1–3.

When U. S. Presidents Took Office

John Adams	Abraham Lincoln	Woodrow Wilson	John F. Kennedy
1797	1861	1913	1961

1 Which person on the time line became President first?

Ⓐ Woodrow Wilson

Ⓑ John Adams

Ⓒ John F. Kennedy

Ⓓ Abraham Lincoln

2 Which person on the time line became President last?

Ⓕ John F. Kennedy

Ⓖ Woodrow Wilson

Ⓗ Abraham Lincoln

Ⓙ John Adams

3 Which person on the time line became President in 1861?

Ⓐ John Adams

Ⓑ John F. Kennedy

Ⓒ Woodrow Wilson

Ⓓ Abraham Lincoln

GO

Directions: Study the map of the United States. Then do numbers 4–7.

4 Which state is a peninsula?

- Ⓕ Nevada
- Ⓖ Florida
- Ⓗ Washington
- Ⓙ Georgia

5 Which state is farthest north?

- Ⓐ Texas
- Ⓑ Arizona
- Ⓒ New York
- Ⓓ Kansas

6 Which state is on the West Coast?

- Ⓕ California
- Ⓖ North Carolina
- Ⓗ Utah
- Ⓙ Minnesota

7 Which state is east of Nebraska?

- Ⓐ Oregon
- Ⓑ Mississippi
- Ⓒ Idaho
- Ⓓ New Mexico

STOP

Lesson 2   Review

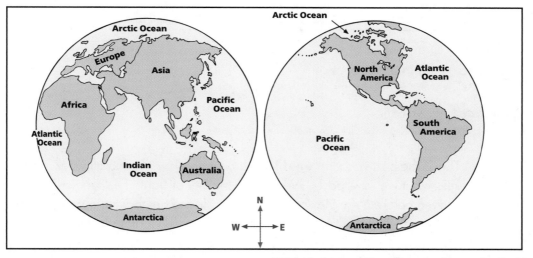

Directions: For numbers 1 and 2, find the answer that best completes each sentence.

1 **The United States is a**

Ⓐ continent.

Ⓑ country.

Ⓒ hemisphere.

Ⓓ state.

2 **A compass rose is**

Ⓕ a type of flower.

Ⓖ an imaginary line around Earth.

Ⓗ a way to tell direction.

Ⓙ a tool for making math shapes.

Directions: Read numbers 3–5. Decide whether each one is true or false.

3 **The land on Earth is divided into seven continents.**

Ⓐ True   Ⓑ False

4 **José and Ling have been studying the southern hemisphere. One of the countries they have likely been studying is France.**

Ⓐ True   Ⓑ False

5 **Muhammad's teacher will travel from the United States to Europe. To reach Europe, he will not have to cross an ocean.**

Ⓐ True   Ⓑ False

GO

Directions: Read the e-mail about a vacation and then do numbers 6–8.

Send To: Ali@internet.com

Subject: my vacation

Dear Ali,

This is the best vacation ever! We've been in New Mexico all week. You'll never guess what we saw today. We went to the city of Santa Fe. Pueblo Indians lived here even before New Mexico was a state. I found out that the Spanish word "pueblo" means "village." I also found out that the Pueblo Indians found a special way to water crops in the heat. They also made pottery and jewelry and wove beautiful baskets. They're still making these things today. I'm bringing a basket back for you. See you soon!

Tyree

6 **Tyree is *most likely* a**

Ⓐ farmer.

Ⓒ Pueblo Indian.

Ⓑ hotel owner in New Mexico.

Ⓓ student.

7 **From the passage, you can tell that Pueblo Indians *probably did not***

Ⓕ work hard.

Ⓗ make bracelets.

Ⓖ grow crops.

Ⓙ live in a cold climate.

8 **The word *pueblo* means**

Ⓐ Indian.

Ⓒ jewelry.

Ⓑ village.

Ⓓ baskets.

STOP

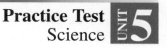

Lesson 1

Directions: Read the Venn diagram, and then do numbers 1–4.

African Elephant
• ears cover shoulder
• back dips
• two finger-like lobes at the end of trunk
• smooth forehead
• wrinkled skin

Both Elephants
• long tusks
• tail
• eat plants

Indian Elephants
• ears do not cover shoulder
• back arches
• one lobe on trunk
• two lumps on forehead
• less wrinkled skin

1 Which elephants have long tusks?

Ⓐ Only the African elephants

Ⓑ Only the Indian elephants

Ⓒ Both the African and Indian elephants

2 Which elephants have one lobe at the end of their trunks?

Ⓕ Only the African elephants

Ⓖ Only the Indian elephants

Ⓗ Both the African and Indian elephants

3 Which elephants have ears that cover their shoulders?

Ⓐ Only the African elephants

Ⓑ Only the Indian elephants

Ⓒ Both the African and Indian elephants

4 Which elephants eat plants?

Ⓕ Only the African elephants

Ⓖ Only the Indian elephants

Ⓗ Both the African and Indian elephants

GO

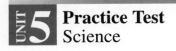
Directions: For numbers 5–7, find each true statement.

5 Ⓐ Chlorophyll is the process in which plants turn water and air into food.

Ⓑ Photosynthesis is the process in which plants turn light, water, and air into food.

Ⓒ Plants need leaves in order to turn water and air into food.

Ⓓ Light is not necessary for plants to turn water and air into food.

6 Ⓕ The seeds take in light and nutrients from the air.

Ⓖ The leaves take in water and nutrients from the soil.

Ⓗ The roots take in water and nutrients from the soil.

Ⓙ The flowers take in light and water from the soil.

7 Ⓐ Conifers (example: pine trees) lose their leaves in the fall.

Ⓑ Conifers stay green year round.

Ⓒ Conifers have broad leaves.

Ⓓ Conifers' leaves turn gold in the fall.

Directions: Do numbers 8–11.

8 Which is not part of a flower?

Ⓕ pistil

Ⓖ stamen

Ⓗ thorax

Ⓙ petal

9 Which part of the flower holds the pollen?

Ⓐ stamen

Ⓑ pistil

Ⓒ sepal

Ⓓ petal

10 Food-making material in leaves is called

Ⓕ chlorophyll.

Ⓖ photosynthesis.

Ⓗ sunlight.

Ⓙ water.

11 Which does a plant not need to grow?

Ⓐ light   Ⓒ soil

Ⓑ water   Ⓓ sand

STOP

Lesson 2 Review

1 **Which is an example of evaporation?**

Ⓐ

Ⓑ

Ⓒ

Ⓓ

Directions: Study the graph of rainfall in Kansas, and then do numbers 5 and 6.

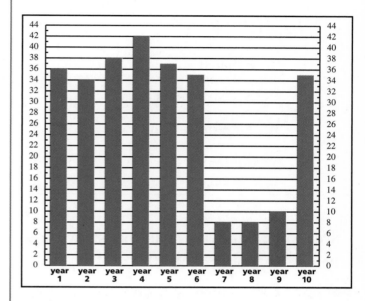

2 **A rainstorm is an example of**

Ⓕ precipitation. Ⓗ condensation.

Ⓖ evaporation. Ⓙ reformulation.

3 **Which of these is not a type of cloud?**

Ⓐ cirrus Ⓒ humerus

Ⓑ cumulus Ⓓ stratus

4 **What does a meteorologist use to measure air pressure?**

Ⓕ barometer Ⓗ odometer

Ⓖ kilometer Ⓙ thermometer

5 **What weather condition is suggested by the rainfall data for years 7–9?**

Ⓐ flood Ⓒ hurricane

Ⓑ tornado Ⓓ drought

6 **Which period of time showed the greatest increase in rainfall?**

Ⓕ from year 2 to year 3

Ⓖ from year 6 to year 7

Ⓗ from year 7 to year 8

Ⓙ from year 9 to year 10

GO

Directions: Do numbers 7 and 8.

7 **Which of the following probably does not add to the greenhouse effect?**

Ⓐ car exhaust

Ⓑ factory smokestacks

Ⓒ airplane pollution

Ⓓ pesticides

8 **A species of animal that has been completely wiped out is**

Ⓕ endangered.

Ⓖ extinct.

Ⓗ hibernating.

Ⓙ migrating.

Directions: Study the chart that shows how much one school has helped the environment. Then do numbers 9 and 10.

Conservation Efforts at Coe School			
Year	Pounds of Paper Recycled	Pounds of Cans Recycled	Number of Trees Planted
1990	550	475	120
2000	620	469	250
2001	685	390	320

9 **Which sentence is true about paper recycling at Coe School?**

Ⓐ Students recycled more paper each year.

Ⓑ Students recycled less paper each year.

Ⓒ Students never recycled paper.

Ⓓ Students recycled the same amount of paper each year.

10 **Which conservation project did not show better results each year?**

Ⓕ recycling paper

Ⓖ recycling cans

Ⓗ planting trees

Ⓙ They all showed better results each year.

STOP

Reading and Language Arts

Find the underlined part of the sentence that is the <u>simple subject</u>.

Two <u>planes</u> flew <u>over</u> our <u>house</u> yesterday <u>morning</u>.

    Ⓐ   Ⓑ   Ⓒ   Ⓓ

Directions: Read this story about a woman pilot and then do numbers 1–7.

THE FORGOTTEN FLYER

More than 80 years ago, Jacqueline Cochran was born to a poor family in Pensacola, Florida. Like many girls at the time, she went to work at an early age. When she was just eight years old, Jacqueline Cochran worked in a cotton mill. Jacqueline went on to do many things in her life, but her great dream was to become an aviator.

When Ms. Cochran became a pilot in the 1930s, flying was still in its infancy. Planes were still new inventions, and only the most daring men flew them. Almost no women were flyers, but that didn't stop Jacqueline. She took flying lessons, and was soon good enough to enter famous races. In 1938, she won first prize in a contest to fly across America.

Near the beginning of World War II, Jacqueline trained women in England to become pilots. She later did the same thing for over a thousand American women. In 1945, she was awarded the Distinguished Service Medal, one of America's highest honors.

When the roar of jet planes replaced the clatter of propeller planes, Jacqueline learned to fly them, and soon was the first woman to fly faster than the speed of sound. Jacqueline also set many other records, including flying higher than anyone had before her.

In many ways, Jacqueline Cochran is the forgotten flyer. But she should be remembered, because this aviation pioneer helped establish flying as one of our most important means of transportation.

GO

1 **What makes Jacqueline Cochran so special?**

  Ⓐ working at an early age

  Ⓑ founding a business

  Ⓒ being an early flyer

  Ⓓ being born in Florida

2 **This story suggests that**

  Ⓕ jets came after propeller planes.

  Ⓖ propeller planes came after jets.

  Ⓗ many people flew in the 1930s.

  Ⓙ Jacqueline Cochran founded an airline.

3 **Another way to say "flying faster than the speed of sound" is**

  Ⓐ making a loud sound.

  Ⓑ breaking the sound barrier.

  Ⓒ flying a loud plane.

  Ⓓ winning an important race.

4 **Look at the picture of Jacqueline Cochran below. The picture shows Jacqueline**

  Ⓕ winning an important award.

  Ⓖ working at a mill.

  Ⓗ with her invention.

  Ⓙ getting ready to fly.

GO

5 The story says that "flying was still in its infancy" when Jacqueline began. What does this probably mean?

Ⓐ It was something new.

Ⓑ She was very young.

Ⓒ Infants could fly.

Ⓓ Planes were small.

6 Cotton is a kind of fabric.

Find another thing that is a fabric.

Ⓕ paper   Ⓗ silk

Ⓖ a comb   Ⓙ shoes

7 *Roar* is a word that sounds like the sound it names. Some other examples are *buzz*, *splash*, and *croak*.

Find another word that sounds like the sound it names.

Ⓐ catch

Ⓑ beep

Ⓒ drive

Ⓓ loud

GO

Directions: For numbers 8 and 9, find the word or words that best complete the sentence.

8 **My sister _____ to Space Camp.**

    Ⓕ gone   Ⓗ go

    Ⓖ going   Ⓙ went

9 **She said it was the _____ she had ever had.**

    Ⓐ funniest   Ⓒ most fun

    Ⓑ more fun   Ⓓ most funner

10 **Find the word that fits both sentences below.**

We _____ at eight o'clock for the lake.
The house on the _____ is mine.

    Ⓕ left   Ⓗ side

    Ⓖ went   Ⓙ right

11 **Find the underlined part of the sentence that is the <u>simple subject</u>.**

A <u>large</u> <u>tree</u> grew <u>beside</u> the <u>lake</u>.
     Ⓐ   Ⓑ   Ⓒ   Ⓓ

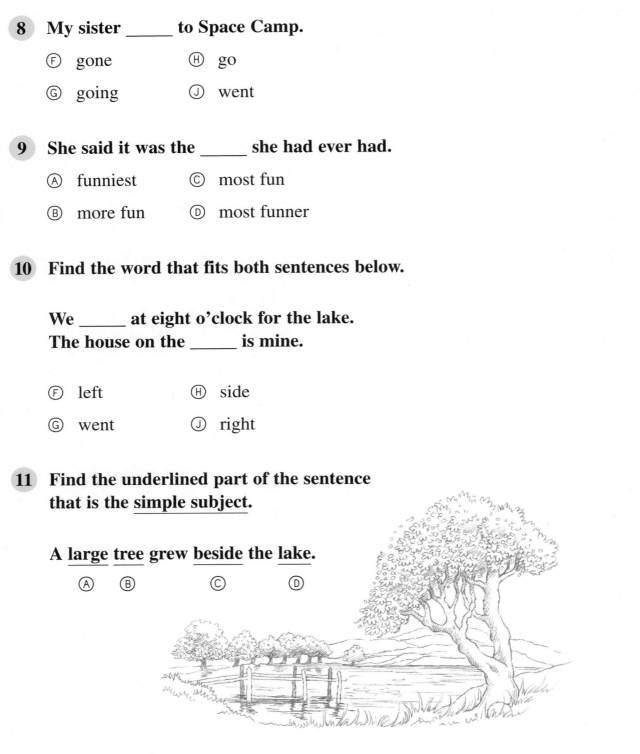

STOP

0:20
Pages 123–125
Time Limit:
approx. 20 minutes

Final Test
Reading and Language Arts   UNIT **1**

Directions: Read the passage. Then, answer numbers 12–21.

Therapy Dogs

Therapy dogs can help patients **recover** from many illnesses. The dogs' owners or handlers bring them into hospital rooms and encourage patients to **interact** with the animals. Dogs sometimes get right up on patients' beds. People who are sick or recovering from surgery pet the dogs, brush them, talk to them, and even allow the friendly pets to **nuzzle** their faces. Studies have shown that interacting with dogs and other animals is highly **therapeutic**: it can **reduce** stress, lower blood pressure, and even promote healing.

Obviously, not all dogs are **well-suited** for this important job. To be a therapy dog, a dog must have a calm, friendly **disposition**. Some therapy dog owners feel their pets were born to help sick people get well.

12 **What is this passage mainly about?**

　Ⓕ　working dogs

　Ⓖ　therapy dogs

　Ⓗ　hospital volunteers

　Ⓙ　friendly pets

13 **Which words help you figure out the meaning of *therapeutic*?**

　Ⓐ　"well-suited for this important job"

　Ⓑ　"interacting with dogs and other animals"

　Ⓒ　"reduce stress, lower blood pressure"

　Ⓓ　"Studies have shown"

14 **Which word is a synonym for *recover*?**

- Ⓕ heal
- Ⓖ sleep
- Ⓗ suffer
- Ⓙ avoid

15 *Nuzzling* **is like**

- Ⓐ rubbing.
- Ⓑ kissing.
- Ⓒ drinking.
- Ⓓ biting.

16 **Which word is not a synonym for *reduce*?**

- Ⓕ shrink
- Ⓖ lessen
- Ⓗ increase
- Ⓙ decrease

17 **When you *interact* with another person, you**

- Ⓐ communicate with him or her.
- Ⓑ copy his or her behavior.
- Ⓒ avoid speaking to him or her.
- Ⓓ tell others about him or her.

18 **A person who is *well-suited* for a certain job is**

- Ⓕ wearing a special uniform.
- Ⓖ able to afford the right clothes for the job.
- Ⓗ someone who can do the job well.
- Ⓙ calm and gentle.

GO

19 *Disposition* means about the same as

Ⓐ breed.

Ⓒ work experience.

Ⓑ personality.

Ⓓ reputation.

20 The writer of the passage mainly wants to

Ⓕ persuade readers to volunteer in hospitals.

Ⓖ entertain readers with some dog stories.

Ⓗ give information about therapy dogs.

Ⓙ give information about one special dog.

21 What kind of dog would probably not make a good therapy dog?

Ⓐ a golden retriever

Ⓒ a dog that lived with children

Ⓑ an older dog

Ⓓ a dog that does not like to be petted

Directions: For numbers 22–25, decide whether each statement is true or false.

22 Therapy dogs are pets that belong to patients.

Ⓐ true

Ⓑ false

23 The writer thinks that bringing therapy dogs into hospitals is a good idea.

Ⓐ true

Ⓑ false

24 No sick person would turn down a visit from a friendly dog.

Ⓐ true

Ⓑ false

25 Interacting with dogs probably makes some patients feel happier and calmer.

Ⓐ true

Ⓑ false

STOP

UNIT 1 **Final Test**
Reading and Language Arts

⌐0:20⌐
Pages 126–128
Time Limit:
approx. 20 minutes

Directions: Read the passage. Then, answer numbers 26–34.

MAKING CLAY MOVE

Beginning in the late 1900s, **claymation** became very popular. **Animators** have used clay animation to make several famous movies and TV commercials. However, claymation is not a new **technique**. In 1897 a clay-like **substance** called plasticine was invented. Moviemakers used plasticine to create clay animation films as early as 1908.

Here's how claymation works. First, an artist makes one or more clay models. Moviemakers **pose** each model, take a camera shot, and stop. Next they move the model a tiny bit (into a very slightly different pose), and **shoot** again. They continue to shoot, move the model, shoot, move the model, and so on. It takes many separate shots to make one second of film.

Today's animators usually use clays such as Sculpey™ or Fimo™. Computer techniques have made the claymation process much less **time-consuming**. However, the basics of clay animation have not changed in almost 100 years!

26 **What is this passage mainly about?**

Ⓕ plasticine

Ⓖ types of clay

Ⓗ claymation techniques and history

Ⓙ famous movies made with claymation

27 **An *animator* is someone who**

Ⓐ creates clay sculptures.

Ⓑ makes animated films.

Ⓒ uses claymation only.

Ⓓ invents clay substances.

28 **The word *claymation* comes from the words *clay* and**

Ⓕ movement.

Ⓖ technician.

Ⓗ concentration.

Ⓙ animation.

29 **Which word means the same as *technique*?**

Ⓐ technical

Ⓑ method

Ⓒ movie

Ⓓ talent

GO

30 **Which word is a synonym for** *substance*?

Ⓤ sound

Ⓠ substitute

Ⓡ liquid

Ⓢ material

31 **What does it mean to** *pose* **something?**

Ⓐ roll it into a ball

Ⓑ squash it flat

Ⓒ use it to make a model

Ⓓ move it into a certain position

32 **In this passage, the word** *shoot* **means**

Ⓤ to fire a gun.

Ⓠ a part of a plant that has just begun to grow.

Ⓡ to take a photograph or make a movie.

Ⓢ to move quickly.

33 **Which word means the opposite of** *time-consuming*?

Ⓐ speedy

Ⓑ sluggish

Ⓒ frustrating

Ⓓ satisfying

34 **The writer of the passage mainly wants to**

Ⓤ persuade readers to rent certain videotapes.

Ⓠ entertain readers with some filmmaking stories.

Ⓡ give information about claymation.

Ⓢ give information about plasticine.

GO

Directions: Choose the correct answer to each question to complete the analogies.

35 <u>Rose</u> is to <u>flower</u> as <u>oak</u> is to _____.

Ⓐ leaf   Ⓒ bush

Ⓑ furniture   Ⓓ tree

36 <u>Begin</u> is to <u>cease</u> as <u>confuse</u> is to _____.

Ⓕ clarify   Ⓗ continue

Ⓖ annoy   Ⓙ stop

37 <u>Supermarket</u> is to <u>groceries</u> as <u>bookstore</u> is to _____.

Ⓐ food   Ⓒ reading materials

Ⓑ paper   Ⓓ library

38 <u>Fork</u> is to <u>eat</u> as <u>ruler</u> is to _____.

Ⓕ cut   Ⓗ spoon

Ⓖ measure   Ⓙ inch

Directions: Match words with the same meanings. Mark the letter of your choice.

39	**frothy**	A	delicious	**39**	Ⓐ Ⓑ Ⓒ Ⓓ
40	**tasty**	B	raw	**40**	Ⓐ Ⓑ Ⓒ Ⓓ
41	**uncooked**	C	foamy	**41**	Ⓐ Ⓑ Ⓒ Ⓓ
42	**spicy**	D	hot	**42**	Ⓐ Ⓑ Ⓒ Ⓓ

Directions: Match words with opposite meanings. Mark the letter of your choice.

43	**polite**	F	backward	**43**	Ⓕ Ⓖ Ⓗ Ⓙ
44	**behind**	G	rude	**44**	Ⓕ Ⓖ Ⓗ Ⓙ
45	**forward**	H	fantastic	**45**	Ⓕ Ⓖ Ⓗ Ⓙ
46	**realistic**	J	ahead	**46**	Ⓕ Ⓖ Ⓗ Ⓙ

STOP

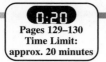

0:20
Pages 129–130
Time Limit:
approx. 20 minutes

Final Test
Writing UNIT **1**

Directions: Read the paragraph that tells how to make a peanut butter and jelly sandwich. Then think of something you like to make or do. Write a paragraph that tells how to make it. Use the words *first*, *next*, *then*, *last*.

These steps tell how to make a peanut butter and jelly sandwich. First get two pieces of bread, peanut butter, jelly, and a knife. Next spread peanut butter on one piece of bread. Then spread jelly on the other piece. Last press the two pieces of bread together.

_____

_____

_____

_____

_____

_____

_____

_____

_____

_____

_____

_____

_____

_____

_____

GO

Directions: Read the letter below. In the letter, a girl explains to her father why she should be allowed to try inline skating. Then think of something you would like to be allowed to do. Write a letter to explain to someone why you should be allowed to do it.

> *Dear Dad,*
>
> *I would like to try inline skating. I know that you think it is not safe, but I would be very careful. I would follow every safety rule. I would wear a helmet, elbow pads, and knee pads. I would only skate in safe places. Please give me a chance.*
>
> *Love,*
>
> *Bonita*

_____

_____

_____

_____

_____

_____

_____

_____

_____

_____

_____

_____

STOP

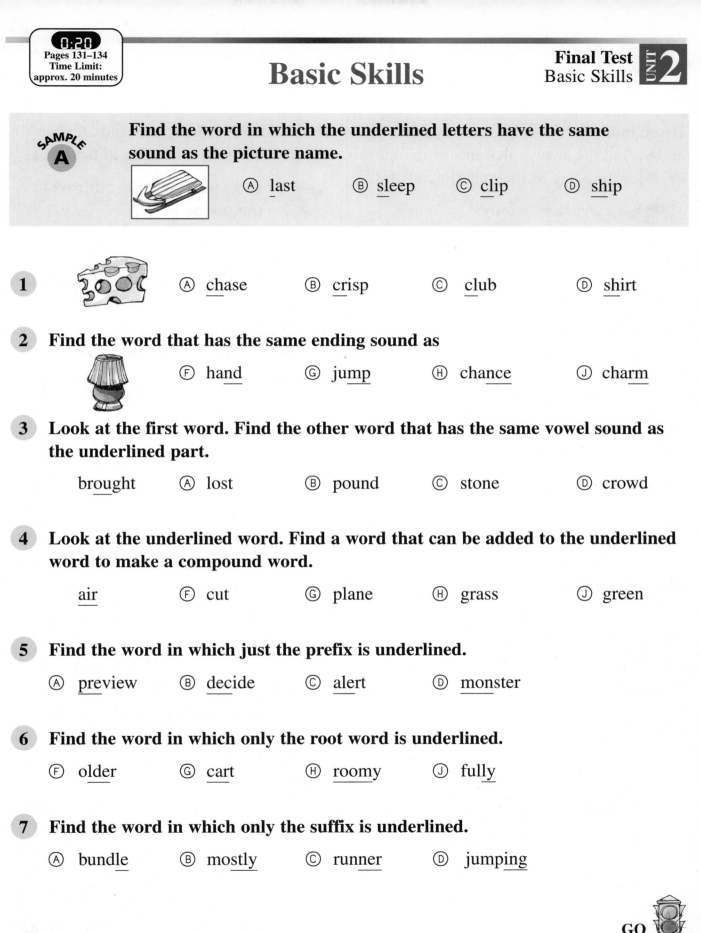

Pages 131–134
Time Limit:
approx. 20 minutes

Basic Skills

Final Test
Basic Skills

UNIT 2

SAMPLE A Find the word in which the underlined letters have the same sound as the picture name.

Ⓐ last   Ⓑ sleep   Ⓒ clip   Ⓓ ship

1   Ⓐ chase   Ⓑ crisp   Ⓒ club   Ⓓ shirt

2 Find the word that has the same ending sound as

Ⓕ hand   Ⓖ jump   Ⓗ chance   Ⓙ charm

3 Look at the first word. Find the other word that has the same vowel sound as the underlined part.

brought   Ⓐ lost   Ⓑ pound   Ⓒ stone   Ⓓ crowd

4 Look at the underlined word. Find a word that can be added to the underlined word to make a compound word.

air   Ⓕ cut   Ⓖ plane   Ⓗ grass   Ⓙ green

5 Find the word in which just the prefix is underlined.

Ⓐ preview   Ⓑ decide   Ⓒ alert   Ⓓ monster

6 Find the word in which only the root word is underlined.

Ⓕ older   Ⓖ cart   Ⓗ roomy   Ⓙ fully

7 Find the word in which only the suffix is underlined.

Ⓐ bundle   Ⓑ mostly   Ⓒ runner   Ⓓ jumping

GO

Directions: For Sample B and numbers 8 and 9, find the answer that means the same or about the same as the underlined word.

SAMPLE B <u>extremely</u> windy

Ⓐ slightly   Ⓒ often

Ⓑ somewhat   Ⓓ very

8 famous <u>legend</u>

Ⓐ person   Ⓒ place

Ⓑ tale   Ⓓ painting

9 <u>create</u> a statue

Ⓕ enjoy   Ⓗ see

Ⓖ make   Ⓙ drop

Directions: For Sample C and number 10, find the answer that best fits in the blank.

SAMPLE C Did you _____ the address in the phone book?

Ⓐ lose   Ⓒ know

Ⓑ find   Ⓓ forget

10 Which word means George's project was in the center of the room?

George's project was in the _____ of the room.

Ⓐ front   Ⓒ middle

Ⓑ back   Ⓓ side

Directions: Find the word that correctly completes both sentences.

11 Use the _____ to make the hole. The _____ team won a prize.

Ⓕ drill   Ⓗ needle

Ⓖ nail   Ⓙ marching

12 This _____ of plant is rare. Mr. Westgate is very _____.

Ⓐ type   Ⓒ nice

Ⓑ kind   Ⓓ happy

Directions: For each blank, look at the words with the same number. Find the word from each list that fits best in the blank.

The bus was more __(13)__ than normal. It was raining hard, and many people who __(14)__ walked to work took the bus today.

13 Ⓕ empty   Ⓗ expensive

Ⓖ crowded   Ⓙ practical

14 Ⓐ never   Ⓒ usually

Ⓑ recently   Ⓓ quickly

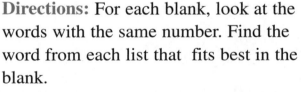

GO

Directions: For Sample D and numbers 15 and 16, find the part of the sentence that needs a capital letter. Mark "None" if no capital letter is needed.

SAMPLE D	a small bird	landed on	the feeder.	None
	Ⓐ	Ⓑ	Ⓒ	Ⓓ

15 We drove | to iowa | last summer. | None
　　　Ⓐ　　　　Ⓑ　　　　　Ⓒ　　　　　　Ⓓ

16 **Find the punctuation mark that is needed in the sentence.** *How long will you be gone?*

.　　　　!　　　　,　　　None
Ⓕ　　　　Ⓖ　　　Ⓗ　　　　Ⓙ

Directions: Find the sentence that has correct capitalization and punctuation.

17 Ⓐ This is a great book

　　Ⓑ Nora gave it to me.

　　Ⓒ i'm almost done.

　　Ⓓ You can have it next?

18 Ⓕ We aren't ready yet.

　　Ⓖ Dont leave without us.

　　Ⓗ The bags are packed? Let's go.

　　Ⓙ The ride to the beach will be an hour

Directions: Read the paragraph. Find the answer that shows the correct capitalization and punctuation for the underlined parts.

(19) *A family of rabbit's visits our yard every day. They eat grass and some flowers. Mom doesn't mind. She says there are plenty of flowers for*
(20) *everyone. The baby rabbits seem to get bigger every day.*

19 Ⓐ rabbit's visit's　　Ⓒ rabbits visits

　　Ⓑ rabbits visit's　　Ⓓ Correct as it is

20 Ⓕ everyone,　　Ⓗ everyone!

　　Ⓖ everyone?　　Ⓙ Correct as it is

GO

Directions: For each question, find the answer choice that shows correct capitalization and punctuation for the underlined words.

21 The soccer match is <u>thursday the</u> baseball game is Friday.

Ⓐ Thursday: the   Ⓒ Thursday. the

Ⓑ Thursday. The   Ⓓ Correct as it is

22 "What a terrifying ride that <u>was."</u> <u>Cried</u> Jake.

Ⓕ was." Cried   Ⓗ was!" Cried

Ⓖ was!" cried   Ⓙ Correct as it is

23 You will need the following <u>materials, Yarn,</u> scissors, cardboard, and paste.

Ⓐ materials; yarn

Ⓑ materials: Yarn

Ⓒ materials: yarn

Ⓓ Correct as it is

24 The traffic reporter <u>announced, all</u> lanes are now closed on Route 22."

Ⓕ announced, "All

Ⓖ announced, "all

Ⓗ announced: "All

Ⓙ Correct as it is

25 <u>Greensburg pennsylvania</u> is about 35 miles east of Pittsburgh.

Ⓐ Greensburg, pennsylvania

Ⓑ Greensburg, Pennsylvania,

Ⓒ Greensburg, Pennsylvania

Ⓓ Correct as it is

26 "<u>Yes, Maggie, you</u> can come over now," said Ann.

Ⓕ "yes, Maggie, you

Ⓖ "Yes Maggie you

Ⓗ "Yes Maggie you,

Ⓙ Correct as it is

27 We <u>washed dried and put</u> away the dishes.

Ⓐ washed, dried, and put

Ⓑ washed dried and, put

Ⓒ washed, dried and put,

Ⓓ Correct as it is

STOP

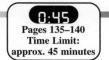

Directions: Read the questions. Mark the letter next to the correct answer. Use the sample index to answer numbers 28–30.

O
Oak, 291-292
Obsidian, 175-176
Oceans, 361-375
   density of, 363-364
   life in, 367-370
   waves, 371-372
   temperature of, 365
   resources, 373-375

28 **You will find information about what topic on page 365?**

   Ⓕ ocean temperatures

   Ⓖ density of the ocean

   Ⓗ waves

   Ⓙ the octopus

29 **On what pages will you most likely find information about mining the oceans for minerals?**

   Ⓐ pages 175-176

   Ⓑ pages 368-369

   Ⓒ pages 373-375

   Ⓓ pages 371-372

30 **You can read about octopuses on pages 368-369. This information is part of what section under Oceans?**

   Ⓕ resources

   Ⓖ life in

   Ⓗ waves

   Ⓙ temperature

Directions: Use the web to answer number 31.

31 **Which of the following belongs on the web?**

   Ⓐ traveling with your pet

   Ⓑ heat exhaustion

   Ⓒ finding a lost pet

   Ⓓ cold weather and your pet

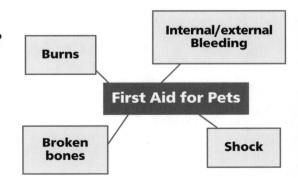

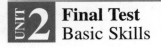

UNIT 2 Final Test
Basic Skills

Directions: Use the sample table of contents to answer numbers 32–33.

Table of Contents

32 In which chapter would you most likely read about otters, seals, and walruses?

Ⓕ Chapter 5
Ⓖ Chapter 1
Ⓗ Chapter 4
Ⓙ Chapter 3

33 Which chapter is the shortest?

Ⓐ Chapter 5
Ⓑ Chapter 2
Ⓒ Chapter 3
Ⓓ Chapter 1

Directions: Find the choice that rhymes with the underlined word.

34 a tough test

Ⓕ cough
Ⓖ rough
Ⓗ laugh
Ⓙ thorough

35 chose a new outfit

Ⓐ lose
Ⓑ news
Ⓒ close
Ⓓ loose

36 Where is the umbrella?

Ⓕ here
Ⓖ were
Ⓗ there
Ⓙ hear

37 the new roof

Ⓐ gruff
Ⓑ truth
Ⓒ wife
Ⓓ aloof

GO

Directions: For numbers 38–41, choose the form of the verb that correctly completes each sentence.

38 **My parents and I _____ to New York tomorrow.**

- Ⓕ flew
- Ⓗ flies
- Ⓖ are flying
- Ⓙ have flown

39 **My father _____ to attend a business conference.**

- Ⓐ have
- Ⓒ having
- Ⓑ haves
- Ⓓ has

40 **While Dad works next week, Mom and I _____ the sights.**

- Ⓕ have seen
- Ⓗ will see
- Ⓖ am seeing
- Ⓙ seen

41 **This time last year we _____ to San Francisco.**

- Ⓐ went
- Ⓒ have gone
- Ⓑ are going
- Ⓓ was going

Directions: For numbers 42–45, choose the answer choice with a usage error. If there are no errors, fill in the last answer choice.

42
- Ⓕ Them cookies we baked are
- Ⓖ really terrible. Even the dog wouldn't
- Ⓗ eat the one I accidentally dropped.
- Ⓙ no errors

43
- Ⓐ The amazed children watched
- Ⓑ as the doe and her fawn
- Ⓒ wandered slow through the yard.
- Ⓓ no errors

44
- Ⓕ I could of done
- Ⓖ that problem
- Ⓗ without your help.
- Ⓙ no errors

45
- Ⓐ I gave the cookies
- Ⓑ to he and she
- Ⓒ because they looked angry.
- Ⓓ no errors

GO

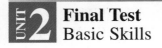
Directions: For numbers 46–48, mark the answer choice that best combines the two sentences.

46 **Marla visited the museum today. Her sister visited the museum today.**

Ⓕ Marla and her sister visited the museum today.

Ⓖ Marla visited and her sister visited the museum today.

Ⓗ Marla visited the museum today and her sister visited the museum today.

Ⓙ Marla visited her sister and the museum today.

47 **Greg attended the concert last night. The concert was in the park.**

Ⓐ The concert last night was in the park Greg attended.

Ⓑ Greg attended last night in the park the concert.

Ⓒ Greg attended the concert last night, and the concert was in the park.

Ⓓ Greg attended the concert in the park last night.

48 **The campers watched as the bear took their food. The campers watched in horror.**

Ⓕ The campers watched as the bear took their food in horror.

Ⓖ The campers in horror watched as the bear took their food.

Ⓗ The campers watched in horror as the bear took their food.

Ⓙ The campers watched as the bear took their food, and the campers were in horror.

Directions: For numbers 49–54, mark the letter of the correctly spelled word that completes each sentence.

49 **On Saturday, I work on my _____.**

Ⓐ hobbies   Ⓒ hobies

Ⓑ hobbys   Ⓓ hobbes

50 **Your sister sings so _____ .**

Ⓕ beautifuly   Ⓗ beautifully

Ⓖ beautyfully   Ⓙ bueatifully

51 **The milk was in a _____.**

Ⓐ picher   Ⓒ pitcher

Ⓑ picture   Ⓓ pitsher

GO

52 We are _____ up by 6:30 a.m. every morning.

- Ⓕ alwase
- Ⓖ always
- Ⓗ allways
- Ⓙ alwaze

53 I hope you're not_____ with your gifts.

- Ⓐ unhappy
- Ⓑ unhapy
- Ⓒ unhappie
- Ⓓ unhappe

54 You should always eat a good _____.

- Ⓕ brekfast
- Ⓖ breakfist
- Ⓗ breakfast
- Ⓙ brakefast

Directions: For numbers 55–60, mark the letter of the underlined word that is misspelled in each sentence. Mark the letter for no errors if all the words are spelled correctly.

55 I <u>wouldn't</u> be the <u>least</u> bit <u>suprised</u> if Jack got here late.   <u>no errors</u>
   Ⓐ   Ⓑ   Ⓒ   Ⓓ

56 <u>Please</u> print your name, <u>adress</u>, and <u>telephone</u> number.   <u>no errors</u>
   Ⓕ   Ⓖ   Ⓗ   Ⓙ

57 The <u>choclate</u> cake you baked is <u>really</u> <u>delicious.</u>   <u>no errors</u>
       Ⓐ   Ⓑ   Ⓒ   Ⓓ

58 I <u>received</u> an <u>invitation</u> to Stan's party next <u>Saturday.</u>   <u>no errors</u>
   Ⓕ   Ⓖ   Ⓗ   Ⓙ

59 Jody has been my best <u>friend</u> <u>sinse</u> we met in <u>first</u> grade.   <u>no errors</u>
                        Ⓐ   Ⓑ   Ⓒ   Ⓓ

60 <u>We're</u> having <u>Thanksgiving</u> dinner with my grandparents <u>tomorow.</u>   <u>no errors</u>
   Ⓕ   Ⓖ   Ⓗ   Ⓙ

GO

Directions: Find the word that is spelled correctly and best fits in the blank.

61 **Let's play _____ it is nice.**

  Ⓐ wheil   Ⓒ while

  Ⓑ wile   Ⓓ wheil

62 **Will you _____ places with me?**

  Ⓕ traid   Ⓗ traed

  Ⓖ tread   Ⓙ trade

63 **An outdoor _____ is near our house.**

  Ⓐ market   Ⓒ marcket

  Ⓑ markit   Ⓓ marked

Directions: Find the underlined word that is not spelled correctly. If all the words are correct, mark "All correct."

64 Ⓕ many friends   Ⓗ feel hungry

  Ⓖ funny joke   Ⓙ All correct

65 Ⓐ among us

  Ⓑ common bird

  Ⓒ fortie minutes

  Ⓓ All correct

Directions: Find the answer that is the solution to the problem. If the answer is not given, choose "None of these."

66

$82 - 35 =$

  Ⓕ 53
  Ⓖ 47
  Ⓗ 57
  Ⓙ 117
  Ⓚ None of these

67

$$\begin{array}{r} \$3.40 \\ +3.60 \\ \hline \end{array}$$

  Ⓐ $.20
  Ⓑ $3.20
  Ⓒ $6.00
  Ⓓ $8.00
  Ⓔ None of these

68

$9 \times 8 =$

  Ⓕ 17
  Ⓖ 64
  Ⓗ 98
  Ⓙ 72
  Ⓚ None of these

69

$$\begin{array}{r} 305 \\ \times 6 \\ \hline \end{array}$$

  Ⓐ 311
  Ⓑ 1830
  Ⓒ 3605
  Ⓓ 3065
  Ⓔ None of these

STOP

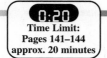
Mathematics

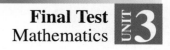
BUILDING OUR CLUBHOUSE

SAMPLE A Which of these is most likely measured in feet?

Ⓐ the distance around a room

Ⓑ the weight of a large box

Ⓒ the distance to the moon

Ⓓ the amount of water in a pool

---

1 Jennie had three bent nails in her pocket. Then she put five straight nails in her pocket. Which answer shows what she had in her pocket?

Ⓐ   Ⓑ   Ⓒ   Ⓓ

---

2 Ricky carried 4 boxes of tiles into the kitchen. Each box held 12 tiles. What would you do to find out how many tiles he carried into the kitchen all together?

add   subtract   divide   multiply

Ⓕ   Ⓖ   Ⓗ   Ⓙ

---

3 Angela wants to measure a piece of wood. Which of these should she use?

Ⓐ   Ⓑ   Ⓒ   Ⓓ

GO

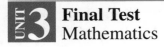
4 Mr. and Mrs. Akers are going to build a deck. It will take 2 weeks to finish. They plan to start on April 24. What date will they finish?

- Ⓕ April 10
- Ⓖ May 1
- Ⓗ April 26
- Ⓙ May 8

5 Pam made this pattern of 4 rows of floor tiles. How many additional gray tiles will be neccessary if she adds 1 more row to make 5 rows of tiles?

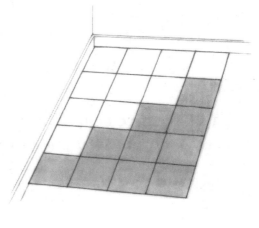

- Ⓐ 5
- Ⓑ 15
- Ⓒ 9
- Ⓓ 20

6 Which pattern of letters could be folded in half on a line of symmetry?

AMOMA	BAGGB	VERDT	UNPOS
Ⓕ	Ⓖ	Ⓗ	Ⓙ

GO

7 The children in the Adams family were stuck inside on a rainy day. They decided to make their own games. They each made a spinner for their game. When Jennie spun her spinner, the color it landed on was gray. Which spinner was probably Jennie's?

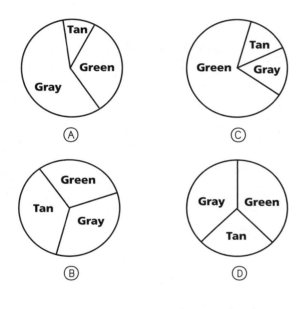

8 This map shows Janelle's yard. She came in through the gate and walked east for 3 yards. Then she went north for 2 yards. What was she closest to?

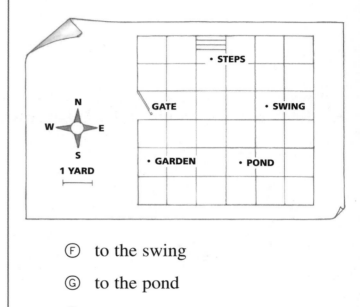

Ⓕ to the swing

Ⓖ to the pond

Ⓗ to the steps

Ⓙ to the garden

9 Rick is carving a pattern in a piece of wood. Which shapes are missing from the pattern?

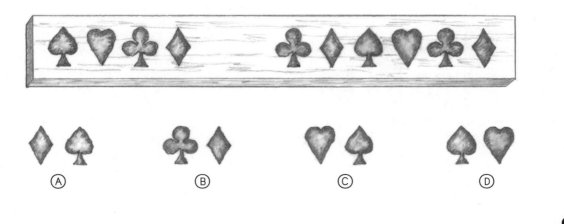

GO

10 **Which of these is not the same shape and size as the others?**

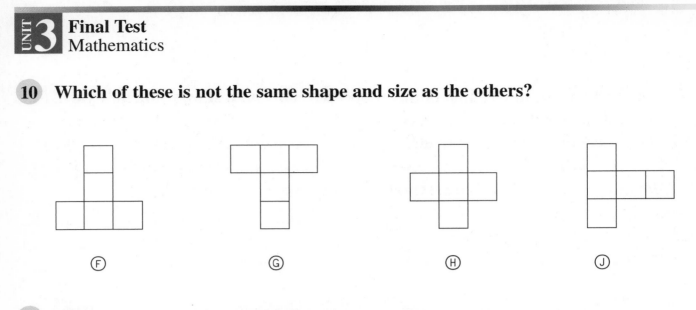

Ⓕ   Ⓖ   Ⓗ   Ⓙ

11 **Look at the group of socks. What fraction of the socks is black?**

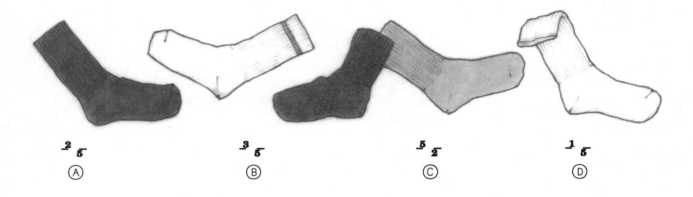

$\frac{2}{5}$ $\frac{3}{5}$ $\frac{5}{2}$ $\frac{1}{5}$

Ⓐ   Ⓑ   Ⓒ   Ⓓ

12 **Look at the graph below and the report Willie made about the coins in his change jar. How many dimes did Willie have in the change jar?**

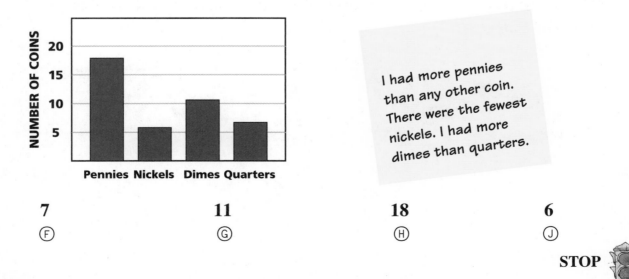

I had more pennies than any other coin. There were the fewest nickels. I had more dimes than quarters.

7   **11**   **18**   **6**

Ⓕ   Ⓖ   Ⓗ   Ⓙ

STOP

Directions: Choose the answer that correctly solves each problem.

13 Which number has a 7 in the ten-thousands place and a 3 in the hundreds place?

Ⓐ 178,234   Ⓒ 498,301

Ⓑ 476,302   Ⓓ 753,092

14 What is the perimeter of the polygon?

Ⓕ 38 inches

Ⓗ 26 inches

Ⓖ 28 inches

Ⓙ not enough information

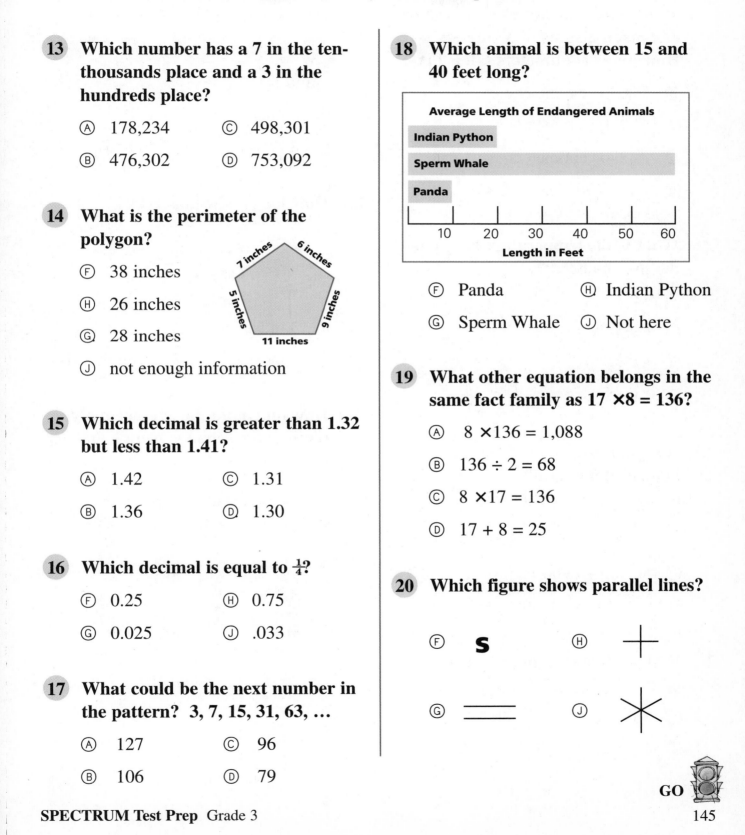

7 inches
6 inches
5 inches
9 inches
11 inches

15 Which decimal is greater than 1.32 but less than 1.41?

Ⓐ 1.42   Ⓒ 1.31

Ⓑ 1.36   Ⓓ 1.30

16 Which decimal is equal to $\frac{1}{4}$?

Ⓕ 0.25   Ⓗ 0.75

Ⓖ 0.025   Ⓙ .033

17 What could be the next number in the pattern? 3, 7, 15, 31, 63, …

Ⓐ 127   Ⓒ 96

Ⓑ 106   Ⓓ 79

18 Which animal is between 15 and 40 feet long?

Average Length of Endangered Animals

Indian Python

Sperm Whale

Panda

10   20   30   40   50   60
Length in Feet

Ⓕ Panda   Ⓗ Indian Python

Ⓖ Sperm Whale   Ⓙ Not here

19 What other equation belongs in the same fact family as 17 ×8 = 136?

Ⓐ 8 ×136 = 1,088

Ⓑ 136 ÷ 2 = 68

Ⓒ 8 ×17 = 136

Ⓓ 17 + 8 = 25

20 Which figure shows parallel lines?

Ⓕ **S**   Ⓗ

Ⓖ   Ⓙ

GO

21 A tsunami is a wave created by underwater earthquakes. Tsunamis can reach heights of 37 meters. How many centimeters tall is that?

Ⓐ 37,000 centimeters

Ⓑ 3,700 centimeters

Ⓒ 370 centimeters

Ⓓ 3.70 centimeters

22 What is the temperature shown on the thermometer?

Ⓕ 74° C

Ⓖ 66° C

Ⓗ 64° C

Ⓙ 54° C

23 How can you write 56,890 in expanded notation?

Ⓐ $5 + 6 + 8 + 9 + 0 =$

Ⓑ $50,000 + 6,000 + 800 + 90 =$

Ⓒ $56,000 + 8900 =$

Ⓓ $0.5 + 0.06 + 0.008 + 0.0009 =$

24 Which number is not a multiple of 4?

Ⓕ 86   Ⓗ 40

Ⓖ 68   Ⓙ 32

25 In a pictograph  stands for 5 books. How many books does

stand for?

Ⓐ 5 books   Ⓒ 20 books

Ⓑ 8 books   Ⓓ 40 books

26 How long is the paperclip?

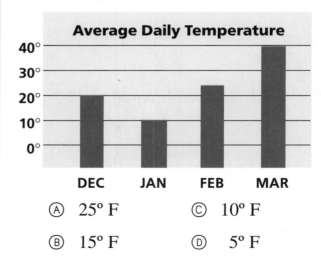

Ⓕ 3 inches   Ⓗ 3 centimeters

Ⓖ 5 inches   Ⓙ 2 centimeters

27 How much did the average daily temperature change from February to March?

Average Daily Temperature

DEC	JAN	FEB	MAR

Ⓐ 25° F   Ⓒ 10° F

Ⓑ 15° F   Ⓓ 5° F

GO

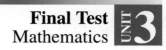

Directions: Choose the answer that correctly solves each problem.

28 8,906 + 3,897 =

Ⓕ 11,803   Ⓗ 12,803

Ⓖ 12,793   Ⓙ 3,893

29 467.902 − 56.894 =

Ⓐ 411.192   Ⓒ 410.192

Ⓑ 411.008   Ⓓ 410.008

30 84 ×.65 =

Ⓕ 44.80   Ⓗ 53.60

Ⓖ 52.80   Ⓙ 54.60

31 $\frac{3}{8} + \frac{1}{8}$ =

Ⓐ 1   Ⓒ $\frac{4}{8}$

Ⓑ $\frac{5}{8}$ Ⓓ $\frac{2}{8}$

32 $\frac{279}{9}$ =

Ⓕ 3   Ⓗ 31

Ⓖ 26   Ⓙ 42

33 $\frac{1}{3} + \frac{2}{3} + 1\frac{1}{3}$ =

Ⓐ $3\frac{2}{3}$ Ⓒ 2

Ⓑ $2\frac{1}{3}$ Ⓓ $1\frac{1}{3}$

34 $\frac{1784}{2}$ =

Ⓕ 876

Ⓖ 892

Ⓗ 1,784

Ⓙ 3,568

35 24.75 + 27.5 + 25.6 =

Ⓐ 77.85

Ⓑ 77.4

Ⓒ 53.10

Ⓓ 50.35

36 4321 + 2987 =

Ⓕ 7,308

Ⓖ 7,208

Ⓗ 7,108

Ⓙ 1,334

37 $\frac{15.05}{5}$ =

Ⓐ 3.01

Ⓑ 3.1

Ⓒ 31

Ⓓ 82

GO

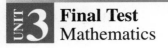
Directions: Choose the answer that correctly solves each problem.

38 Michael was at a card convention. At the first booth he bought 8 cards. He bought 6 cards at each of the remaining 9 booths. How many cards did Michael buy altogether?

Ⓕ 54 cards   Ⓗ 57 cards

Ⓖ 62 cards   Ⓙ 72 cards

39 There were 85 boxes shipped to the warehouse. In each box there were 22 cartons. In each carton there were 40 water guns. How many water guns are in all 85 boxes?

Ⓐ 880 water guns

Ⓑ 1,870 water guns

Ⓒ 74,800 water guns

Ⓓ Not enough information

40 Mary measured the length of a room at 8 feet. How many inches long is the room?

Ⓕ 12 inches

Ⓖ 24 inches

Ⓗ 96 inches

Ⓙ None of these

41 Mr. Thomas bought 2 adult tickets and 1 child ticket to the amusement park. How much money did he spend altogether?

Ⓐ $44.85   Ⓒ $29.90

Ⓑ $38.85   Ⓓ $23.90

42 Rita left dance class at 3:30 p.m. She arrived home at 4:17 p.m. How long did it take Rita to get home?

Ⓕ 1 hour, 17 minutes

Ⓖ 47 minutes

Ⓗ 37 minutes

Ⓙ 13 minutes

STOP

Pages 149–150
Time Limit:
approx. 15 minutes

Social Studies

Final Test UNIT 4
Social Studies

Directions: Choose the best answer for numbers 1–6.

1 **The Boston Tea Party happened because**

Ⓐ workers didn't like to sail.

Ⓑ people believed the tax on tea was not fair.

Ⓒ bosses wanted to take a break and have fun.

Ⓓ settlers needed to move to a new town.

2 **The first President of the United States was**

Ⓕ John Adams

Ⓖ Thomas Jefferson

Ⓗ George Washington

Ⓙ Abraham Lincoln

3 **Which *probably* did not happen because of the invention of the steam engine?**

Ⓐ People visited other states more often.

Ⓑ Children had fewer school days.

Ⓒ Businesses sent their goods across the country.

Ⓓ Workers had new jobs.

4 **Who *probably* made the first United States flag?**

Ⓕ Betsy Ross

Ⓖ John Hancock

Ⓗ Benjamin Franklin

Ⓙ Dolly Madison

5 **What invention helped clean raw cotton?**

Ⓐ sewing machine

Ⓑ slaves

Ⓒ cotton gin

Ⓓ the plow

6 **What *probably* helped pioneers decide to go to California?**

Ⓕ There were big cities there.

Ⓖ There were no Indians.

Ⓗ Travel was safe and cheap.

Ⓙ Gold was discovered there.

GO

Product Map of Midwestern States

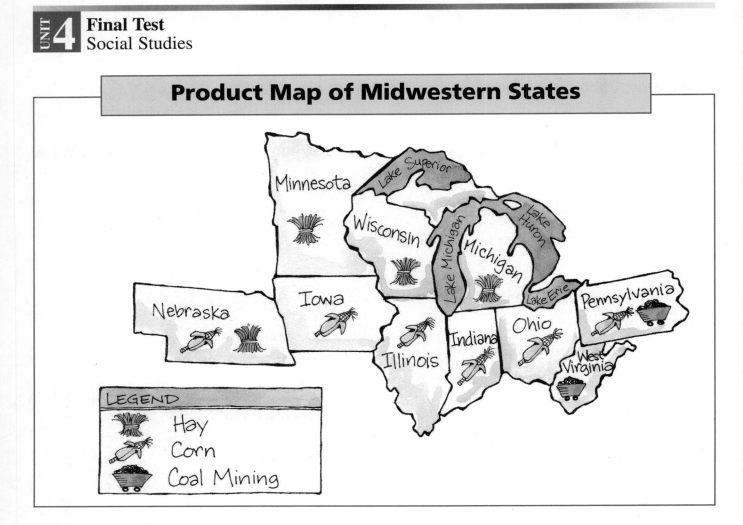

7 **Which state does *not* grow hay?**

Ⓐ Wisconsin

Ⓒ Illinois

Ⓑ Minnesota

Ⓓ Michigan

8 **You would find coal mines in**

Ⓕ Illinois and Pennsylvania.

Ⓗ Iowa and Nebraska.

Ⓖ West Virginia and Indiana.

Ⓙ Pennsylvania and West Virginia.

9 **Which state grows both hay and corn?**

Ⓐ Ohio

Ⓒ Iowa

Ⓑ Nebraska

Ⓓ Wisconsin

STOP

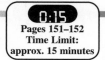
Pages 151–152
Time Limit:
approx. 15 minutes

Science

Final Test
Science UNIT 5

Directions: Do numbers 1–6.

1 What kind of scientist studies rocks and minerals?

Ⓐ biologist

Ⓑ botanist

Ⓒ archeologist

Ⓓ geologist

2 A rock that was formed by volcanic activity is called

Ⓕ sedimentary.

Ⓖ igneous.

Ⓗ metamorphic.

Ⓙ mineral.

3 A sedimentary rock is often formed in a

Ⓐ river bed.

Ⓑ volcano.

Ⓒ mesa.

Ⓓ plateau.

4 A scientist scratches a mineral sample with her fingernail, a penny, and then a nail. What property is she testing?

Ⓕ shininess

Ⓖ chemical make-up

Ⓗ weight

Ⓙ hardness

5 The outermost layer of the Earth is called the

Ⓐ outer core.

Ⓑ inner core.

Ⓒ crust.

Ⓓ mantle.

6 A sudden movement of the Earth's crust is known as

Ⓕ a volcano.

Ⓖ an earthquake.

Ⓗ a hurricane.

Ⓙ a tornado.

GO

Directions: Read the diagram, and then do numbers 7 and 8.

Before   **After**

7 **Which principle is shown in the diagram?**

Ⓐ evaporation

Ⓑ displacement

Ⓒ metamorphosis

Ⓓ isolation

8 **What would happen if the rock in Picture 2 were small instead of large?**

Ⓕ The water level would be higher.

Ⓖ The water would have evaporated.

Ⓗ The water level would be lower.

Ⓙ The water level would be the same.

Directions: Read the graph, and then do numbers 9 and 10.

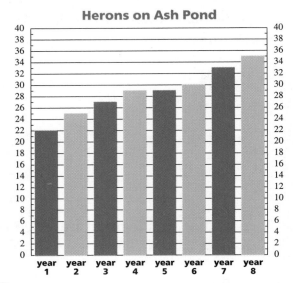

Herons on Ash Pond

9 **In which two years did the number of herons stay the same?**

Ⓐ years 1 and 2

Ⓑ years 2 and 3

Ⓒ years 3 and 4

Ⓓ years 4 and 5

10 **Based on the data, what could you predict for year 11?**

Ⓕ The number of herons will increase.

Ⓖ The number of herons will decrease.

Ⓗ The number of herons will stay the same.

Ⓙ Herons will become endangered.

STOP

Grade 3 Answer Key

Page 26
1. B
2. F
3. B
4. J
5. D
6. G
7. C

Page 28
1. B
2. H
3. D
4. F
5. B
6. H
7. D
8. H
9. B
10. G

Page 30
1. A
2. A
3. B
4. B
5. A
6. B
7. A
8. A
9. A
10. B
11. A
12. B
13. B
14. A

Page 32
1. B
2. D
3. A
4. C
5. J
6. G
7. F
8. H
9. C
10. A
11. B
12. D
13. H
14. G
15. F
16. J

Page 34
1. C
2. G
3. D
4. H
5. B
6. J
7. A
8. F
9. B
10. F

Page 36

FIRST QUESTION: Possible response: They fought against Great Britain.

SECOND QUESTION: Possible response: They wanted their freedom from Great Britain's rule.

THIRD QUESTION: Hot air rises.

FOURTH QUESTION: Gravity brings the balloon to Earth.

FIFTH QUESTION: Possible response: They were scared.

SIXTH QUESTION: Possible response: He took charge and put the fire out.

Page 38
1. B
2. F
3. A
4. H

Page 40
Responses will vary.

Page 43
1. C
2. J
3. B
4. H
5. B
6. H
7. A
8. J

Page 44
9. D
10. G
11. C
12. G
13. D
14. H
15. C

Grade 3 Answer Key

Page 46
1. A
2. H
3. B

Page 48
1. C
2. F; Extra information: 36 oranges, 24 bananas
3. A
4. J

Page 50
1. B
2. F
3. C
4. H

Page 52
1. A
2. G
3. B
4. J
5. C

Page 54
1. B
2. F
3. C
4. G
5. D

Page 56
1. D
2. H
3. D
4. G
5. B

Page 58
1. C
2. F
3. B
4. F
5. D

Page 60
1. B
2. J
3. C
4. J
5. C
6. G
7. A
8. H

Page 62
1. C
2. H
3. C
4. H
5. C
6. J

Page 64
1. C
2. F
3. B
4. F
5. C
6. H

Page 68
1. B
2. H
3. D
4. G
5. C
6. J

Page 69
7. C
8. F

Page 72
1. B
2. H
3. D
4. F

Page 75
A. B
B. F

Page 77
1. C
2. F

Page 78
3. B
4. H
5. C
6. F
7. B

Page 80
8. F
9. C

Page 81
10. J
11. B
12. H

Page 82
A. A
1. A
2. H

Page 83
3. A
4. G
5. C
6. F
7. B

Page 84
8. J
9. B
10. F
11. C
12. F
13. D

Page 85
Responses will vary.

Page 86
FIRST QUESTION: Possible response: It is Juan. He is nervous about seeing his friend, because he hasn't seen him in 6 months.

SECOND QUESTION: Possible response: The story doesn't say where the story takes place. It doesn't really matter.

THIRD QUESTION: Possible response:He is afraid that it won't be the same, but the friend puts him at ease.

Page 87
A. C

Page 88
1. D
2. G
3. A
4. H

Page 89
5. C
6. G
7. A

Grade 3 Answer Key

Page 90
8. H
9. D
10. H
11. A

Page 91
Responses will vary.

Page 92
A. A
1. A
2. G
3. B
4. J

Page 93
A. B
B. F
1. A
2. J
3. C
4. F
5. C

Page 94
C. B
6. D
7. F
8. A
9. J

Page 95
A. B
1. A
2. H
B. C
3. C
4. J

Page 96
5. D
6. H
C. B
7. C
8. J

Page 97
1. A
2. J
3. B
4. G
5. C
A. D
6. B
7. J
8. C

Page 98
A. C
B. K
1. D
2. K
3. A
4. G

Page 99
A. A
1. C
2. H
3. D
4. G
5. D
6. G
7. A

Page 100
B. D
8. B
9. G
C. A
10. C
11. J
12. A
13. H
14. C

Page 101
D. D
15. A
16. G
17. D
18. G
19. C
20. J

Page 102
E. B
21. C
22. H
23. D
24. F
F. D
25. C
26. G
27. B

Page 103
A. C

Page 104
1. B
2. F
3. D
4. F
5. B

Page 105
6. F
7. D
8. F
9. B
10. F
11. C

Page 106
12. F
13. B
14. J

Page 107
15. D
16. J
17. A

Page 108
A. C
1. D
2. G

Page 109
3. B
4. J
5. A
6. J

Page 110
7. C
8. J
9. A

Page 111
1. B
2. F
3. D

Page 112
4. G
5. C
6. F
7. B

Page 113
1. B
2. H
3. A
4. B
5. B

Page 114
6. D
7. J
8. B

Page 115
1. C
2. G
3. A
4. H

Grade 3 Answer Key

Page 116
5. B
6. H
7. B
8. H
9. A
10. F
11. D

Page 117
1. B
2. F
3. C
4. F
5. D
6. J

Page 118
7. D
8. G
9. A
10. G

Page 119
A. A

Page 120
1. C
2. F
3. B
4. J

Page 121
5. A
6. H
7. B

Page 122
8. J
9. C
10. F
11. B

Page 123
12. G
13. C

Page 124
14. F
15. A
16. H
17. A
18. H

Page 125
19. B
20. H
21. D
22. B
23. A
24. B
25. A

Page 126
26. H
27. B
28. J
29. B

Page 127
30. J
31. D
32. H
33. A
34. H

Page 128
35. D
36. F
37. C
38. G
39. C
40. A
41. B
42. D
43. G
44. J
45. F
46. H

Page 129
Responses will vary.

Page 130
Responses will vary.

Page 131
A. B
1. A
2. G
3. A
4. G
5. A
6. H
7. D

Page 132
B. D
8. B
9. G
C. B
10. C
11. F
12. B
13. G
14. C

Page 133
D. A
15. B
16. J
17. B
18. F
19. C
20. J

Page 134
21. B
22. G
23. C
24. H
25. C
26. J
27. A

Page 135
28. F
29. C
30. G
31. B

Page 136
32. G
33. A
34. G
35. C
36. H
37. D

Page 137
38. G
39. D
40. H
41. A
42. F
43. C
44. F
45. B

Page 138
46. F
47. D
48. H
49. A
50. H
51. C

Grade 3 Answer Key

Page 139
52. G
53. A
54. H
55. C
56. G
57. A
58. J
59. B
60. H

Page 140
61. C
62. J
63. A
64. J
65. C
66. G
67. E
68. J
69. B

Page 141
A. A
1. C
2. J
3. B

Page 142
4. J
5. A
6. F

Page 143
7. A
8. H
9. D

Page 144
10. H
11. A
12. G

Page 145
13. B
14. F
15. B
16. F
17. A
18. H
19. C
20. G

Page 146
21. B
22. H
23. B
24. F
25. D
26. H
27. B

Page 147
28. H
29. B
30. J
31. C
32. H
33. B
34. G
35. A
36. F
37. A

Page 148
38. G
39. C
40. H
41. B
42. G

Page 149
1. B
2. H
3. B
4. F
5. C
6. J

Page 150
7. C
8. J
9. B

Page 151
1. D
2. G
3. A
4. J
5. C
6. G

Page 152
7. B
8. H
9. D
10. F

Record Your Scores

After you have completed and checked each test, record your scores below. Do not count your answers for the sample questions or the writing pages.

Practice Test

Unit 1 Reading
Number of Questions: 36   Number Correct _____

Unit 2 Basic Skills
Number of Questions: 60   Number Correct _____

Unit 3 Mathematics
Number of Questions: 26   Number Correct _____

Unit 4 Social Studies
Number of Questions 15   Number Correct _____

Unit 5 Science
Number of Questions: 21   Number Correct _____

Final Test

Unit 1 Reading
Number of Questions: 46   Number Correct _____

Unit 2 Basic Skills
Number of Questions: 69   Number Correct _____

Unit 3 Mathematics
Number of Questions: 42   Number Correct _____

Unit 4 Social Studies
Number of Questions: 9   Number Correct _____

Unit 5 Science
Number of Questions: 10   Number Correct _____

NOTES

NOTES